Demonetisation

Demonetisation

The Economists Speak

Editor

Uma Kapila

ACADEMIC FOUNDATION
NEW DELHI

www.academicfoundation.org

First published in 2017
by

ACADEMIC FOUNDATION
4772-73 / 23 Bharat Ram Road, (23 Ansari Road),
Darya Ganj, New Delhi - 110 002 (India).
Phones : 23245001 / 02 / 03 / 04.
Fax : +91-11-23245005.
E-mail : books@academicfoundation.com
www.academicfoundation.org

Disclaimer:
The findings/views/opinions expressed in this book are solely those of the authors and do not necessarily reflect the views of the publisher.

Demonetisation : the economists speak / editor, Uma Kapila.
pages cm
Contributed articles.
ISBN 9789332703971

1. Monetary policy--India. 2. India--Economic conditions--21st century. I. Kapila, Uma, editor.

HC435.3.D46 2017 DDC 332.4954 23

Typeset, printed and bound by The Book Mint, New Delhi.
www.thebookmint.in

CONTENTS

About the Editor/Contributors

Editor:

Uma Kapila has taught Indian Economy to undergraduate students for over forty-two years. She retired as Reader from the Department of Economics, Miranda House, University of Delhi. Presently, she is Senior Editor, Academic Foundation. An Honours Graduate from Miranda House, University of Delhi and MA and PhD from Delhi School of Economics, Dr Uma Kapila has also served on the Planning Commission Study Group on "Agricultural Strategies in the Eastern Region of India for the Seventh Five Year Plan" (Perspective Planning Division). She is the author of the book *Oilseeds Economy of India* (1982) published by the Institute of Economic Growth, Delhi. She is also the author/editor of textbooks on Indian economy and has edited, and co-edited with Raj Kapila, a number of books on India's economy, banking and finance.

Contributors:

Yoginder K. Alagh is Chancellor of the Central University of Gujarat and Professor Emeritus/Vice-Chair Sardar Patel Institute of Economic and Social Research in Ahmedabad. Earlier he was the Minister of State (Independent Charge) for Planning and Programme Implementation, Science, Technology and Power (1996 to 1998) and Member of the Rajya Sabha (until 2001). He was Vice-Chancellor, Jawaharlal Nehru University, Member Planning Commission, Chairman BICP and Secretary to the Government and Chairman APC. Dr Alagh's professional experience is related to research, policy-making and administration of large research/policy formulation professional groups relating to macro policy and planning, industrial policies and reform, and agricultural planning and policy. He holds a doctorate in Economics from the University of Pennsylvania at Philadelphia. He is extensively published in India and abroad and writes a column for the Express Group and the *Business Line*.

Praveen Chakravarty is a Senior Fellow in Political Economy at the Mumbai think tank, IDFC Institute. He is a prolific writer on economic policy and the political economy of India with many published opinion pieces in all leading mainlines and publications. He spent two decades in the financial services sector across India and the US. Subsequently, he worked with the Unique Identity Authority of India (UIDAI) and the National Skills Development Agency (NSDA). Chakravarty is the Founding Trustee of IndiaSpend, India's first non-profit data journalism initiative. He holds an MBA from the Wharton School.

Bibek Debroy is an economist and was educated in Ramakrishna Mission School, Narendrapur; Presidency College, Kolkata; Delhi School of Economics and Trinity College, Cambridge. Presently he is Member, NITI Aayog, Government of India. He has worked in Presidency College, Kolkata (1979-1983), Gokhale Institute of Politics and Economics, Pune (1983-1987); Indian Institute of Foreign Trade, Delhi (1987-1993); as the Director of a Ministry of Finance/UNDP project on legal reforms (1993-1998); Department of Economic Affairs (1994-95); National Council of Applied Economic Research (1995-96); Rajiv Gandhi Institute for Contemporary Studies (1997-2005); PHD Chamber of Commerce and Industry (2005-06); and Centre for Policy Research (2007-2015). He has authored/edited several books, papers and popular articles and has also been a Consulting/Contributing Editor with several newspapers.

Nitin Desai joined TERI as Distinguished Fellow after a long and illustrious career with the Government of India and the United Nations. A graduate of the London School of Economics, he retired from the UN in 2003 as Under-Secretary General for Economic and Social Affairs. Prior joining the UN, he was Secretary and Chief Economic Adviser in India's Ministry of Finance. He has been associated with many Committees of the Government of India including the National Security Advisory Board, the Prime Minister's Council on Climate Change, and several Committees set up by the Planning Commission, the Ministry of Environment and Forests and the Reserve Bank of India. Mr Desai is an Honorary Professor at the Indian Council for Research in International Economic Relations, a Trustee of the Delhi Policy Group, an Honorary Fellow of the London School of Economics and Political Science, UK. He writes a monthly column for the Indian financial daily, *The Business Standard*.

Rajiv Kumar is Chancellor of the Gokhale Institute of Economics and Politics in Pune, Senior Fellow at the Centre for Policy Research in New Delhi and the Founding Director of Pahle India Foundation. He was previously Secretary General of Federation of Indian Chambers of Commerce and Industry; Director & Chief Executive of Indian Council for Research on International Economic Relations; and Chief Economist of Confederation of Indian Industry (2004-2006). He worked at the Asian Development Bank from 1995 to 2005 and in the Government of India from 1989 to 1995. He is a leading columnist and has published extensively. His latest book, *Modi and his Challenges* was published in May 2016 by Bloomsbury. He has a DPhil in Economics from Oxford University and a PhD from Lucknow University.

Radhika Pandey, PhD in Economics, is consultant with the Macro-Finance Group at the National Institute of Public Finance and Policy, New Delhi. Her core areas of work are macroeconomics, financial sector legislative reforms and capital controls and business cycles. One of the key areas of her work has been to improve measurement of the economy through a research programme on empirical macroeconomics which includes identifying well-measured data, seasonal adjustment and identifying and dating business cycle conditions. She was part of the research team for a number of Ministry of Finance instituted expert committees such as Financial Legislative Reforms Commission (FSLRC), Panel on External Commercial Borrowings and Report of the Working Group on Foreign Investments in India.

Ila Patnaik is a professor at the National Institute of Public Finance and Policy, New Delhi. Prior to this, she was the Principal Economic Advisor to the Government of India. Other recent former positions include Non-Resident Senior Associate at Carnegie Endowment for International Peace, and regular columnist at the *Indian Express*. She holds a BA (Economics) from Delhi University, an MA (Economics) from Jawaharlal Nehru University, and a PhD (Economics) from the University of Surrey. Her research interests include international macroeconomics, finance and emerging economy business cycles. Her works have been published in scholarly journals such as the *Journal of International Money and Finance, the World Bank Economic Review, International Finance*, and in collected volumes. Dr Patnaik served on various working groups and task forces of the Ministry of Finance.

T.C.A. Srinivasa-Raghavan is columnist for *Business Standard* and *The Quint* (Hindi). He has earlier worked in *Financial Express, Indian Express, Economic Times, The Hindu Business Line*. and *Business Standard* where he was in charge of the opinion pages. Raghavan has also been a consultant to the Reserve Bank of India's history project, advisor to the Director of ICRIER, editor of Margin at NCAER and a senior fellow of the Asian Institute of Transport. He is a Distinguished Fellow of the Institute of Peace and Conflict Studies. He has been a Visiting Fellow at Oxford (1990), Cambridge (1983) and at the Delhi School of Economics, Delhi University (1999). He has an MA in economics from the Delhi School of Economics.

Suyash Rai is Senior Consultant at the National Institute of Public Finance and Policy, New Delhi. He has previously worked with ICICI Bank and IFMR Trust. He has served on two government committees, and provided research and advisory support to various policymaking projects. He has consulted with the World Bank and other organisations. His writings have appeared in various popular media publications, such as the *Wall Street Journal, Mint, Hindu Business Line*, etc.

M. Govinda Rao was a Member of the Fourteenth Finance Commission (2013-14). Prior to that, he was the Director, National Institute of Public Finance and Policy (2003-2013), Director, Institute for Social and Economic Change, Bangalore (1998-2002), and Fellow, Research School of Pacific and Asian Studies, Australian National University, Canberra, Australia. He was a Member of the Economic Advisory Council to the Prime Minister (2004-2013), Member of Financial Sector Legislative Reforms Commission (FSLRC); Member, High Level Expert Committee on Universal Health Coverage; Member, High Level Expert Committee on Efficient Management of Public Expenditure. His research interests include: tax policy and reforms, public expenditure management, state and local finance, fiscal decentralisation and federalism. Dr Rao is presently Emeritus Professor, National Institute of Public Finance and Policy.

S.L. Rao is presently a columnist in the *Financial Express* and the *Telegraph* (Calcutta), Distinguished Fellow, Emeritus, The Energy and Resources Institute, (TERI). He is an economist by training and has worked as a professional manager for 28 years in marketing and general management positions in Lever, Warner Hindustan and Bardsell. He was Director-General of NCAER (National Council of Applied Economic Research) from 1990 to 1996; from 1998 to 2001 was the first Chairman of the Central Electricity Regulatory Commission. He was Chairman of the Institute for Social and Economic Change, Bangalore, (2004 to 2010), President, All India Management Association, (1985-86), Vice-President, People's Union for Civil Liberties, Tamil Nadu, (1976-1979). He has authored or edited sixteen books, many papers and hundreds of articles.

C.S.C. Sekhar is a Professor at the Institute of Economic Growth, University of Delhi. His research and teaching interests include: agricultural markets (market structure, price formation, exports, and imports), food security, WTO issues related to agriculture, agricultural growth, rural development, political economy of development and issues related to governance. He is mainly engaged in empirical work using econometric modelling. He is PhD (Economics) from Delhi School of Economics, University of Delhi.

Rajeswari Sengupta is an Assistant Professor of Economics at the Indira Gandhi Institute of Development Research (IGIDR), Mumbai. She holds a Bachelors degree in Economics from Presidency College, Calcutta, a Masters from Delhi School of Economics, and completed her MA and PhD in Economics from the University of California, Santa Cruz (UCSC). Her research focuses on policy-relevant issues of emerging economies in general and India in particular, in the fields of international finance, open economy macroeconomics, monetary policy, and financial markets and regulations. In the past she has held research positions at the Institute for Financial Management and Research, Chennai; Reserve Bank of India, Delhi; and the World Bank and the International Monetary Fund, Washington DC. She has published in reputed international journals such as *Journal of International Money and Finance, The World Economy, Emerging Markets Review, Pacific Economic Review,* and *Open Economies Review* as well as the *Economic and Political Weekly in India*.

Ajay Shah studied at IIT, Bombay and USC, Los Angeles. He has held positions at the Centre for Monitoring Indian Economy (Mumbai), Indira Gandhi Institute for Development Research (Bombay) and the Ministry of Finance, and now works at National Institute of Public Finance and Policy (NIPFP). His research interests include: policy issues on Indian economic growth, open economy macroeconomics, public finance, financial economics and pensions. In the past decade, Prof Shah was extensively involved in the policy process in the reforms of the equity market and the New Pension System.

Mihir S. Sharma was trained as an economist and political scientist in Delhi and in Boston. From 2008, he edited and wrote a column for the opinion pages of *The Indian Express* and *Business Standard*, both based in New Delhi, and has won a Sriram Sanlam award for financial journalism. His book *Restart: The Last Chance for the Indian Economy* was published in 2015, to considerable critical acclaim; it won the Tata LitLive best Business Book of the Year and was longlisted for the Financial Times–McKinsey Business Book of the Year. He is also the India columnist for *Bloomberg View*.

Parthasarathi Shome is Chairman, International Tax Research and Analysis Foundation (ITRAF), Bengaluru. Prior to that he was Adviser (Minister of State) to the Indian Finance Minister, and Chief Economist, Her Majesty's Revenue and Customs (HMRC), United Kingdom. Earlier he was Chief of Tax Policy, International Monetary Fund (IMF), and Professor of Economics, The American University, Washington DC. He received the highest civilian honour of the Brazilian Government, *Commander of the Order of the Southern Cross*, and the Jeanne S. Mattersdorf Award of the National Tax Association of America as "an outstanding student in the field of taxation and public finance" for his PhD thesis from Southern Methodist University.

Manmohan Singh, former Prime Minister of India, is also the only prime minister after Jawaharlal Nehru to return to power after completing a full five-year term. He is rightly acclaimed as a thinker and a scholar and is well regarded for his diligence and his academic approach to work, as well as his unassuming demeanour. During his tenure as finance minister in the Narasimha Rao government (1991 to 1996), he was the mastermind behind the economic liberalisation in India and his role in ushering in a comprehensive policy of economic reforms is recognised worldwide. An economist by profession, among the many Governmental positions that Dr Singh has occupied are Economic Advisor in the Commerce Ministry; Chief Economic Advisor in the Ministry of Finance; Secretary in the Ministry of Finance; Deputy Chairman of the Planning Commission; Governor of the Reserve Bank of India; Advisor of the Prime Minister; and Chairman of the University Grants Commission.

Bhargavi Zaveri is a Senior Research Associate at the Finance Research Group, Indira Gandhi Institute of Development Research, Mumbai. She works in the areas of financial regulation and policy. She has held research positions at the National Institute of Public Finance and Policy, New Delhi and the Harvard Law School. She has advised the Ministry of Finance on issues relating to financial regulation, including foreign capital flows and securities markets. She was part of the team working on the Indian Financial Code and the recently enacted Bankruptcy Code. A lawyer by training, Bhargavi has previously worked at a Mumbai-based law firm for six years, where she advised on corporate and transactional laws.

Acknowledgements

I am extremely grateful to all the contributors who spontaneously responded to my request for inclusion of their articles in the book. My special thanks to Prof Ajay Shah, who through his blog connected me to Radhika, Bhargavi, Praveen, Rajeswari and Suyash. I would also like to thank the editors of *The Hindu*, the *Business Standard*, the *Financial Express* and the *Indian Express* for granting me permission to reproduce the papers published in their dailies.

UMA KAPILA

Introduction

PRIME Minister Narendra Modi on 8th November 2016 made the drastic announcement of demonetising ₹500 and ₹1000 notes. What compelled Modi to take this measure under which 86.4 per cent of the total value of the currency in circulation as of March 2016 became redundant overnight? In seeking public support for demonetisation, he argued it was indispensable to combat: (i) black money, (ii) terrorist financing, and (iii) counterfeit currency. Belatedly, another rationale emerged when these proved untenable—accelerating a shift to a 'less cash/cashless economy'.

Wherever you go, you come across animated discussion on 'demonetisation'. Different groups of people are seen discussing it according to their respective level of intellect, awareness, social and economic background. Much has been written and expressed about demonetisation through all forms of communication medium—conventional, electronic and of course the all pervasive social media. I have been closely following the discussions, debates and writings on the subject which motivated me to bring together a selection of writings by scholars and economists in order to offer the readers a balanced, structured and authentic analysis of the issue in a reader-friendly format.

The book is a collection of 20 articles by 18 economists/scholars and policymakers discussing and giving their perspective on the demonetisation decision.

Bibek Debroy (ch.1) citing legislations and studies relating to demonetisation in India as well as other countries clarifies that demonetisation drive is not meant to address creation of new 'black' income. For that the government has already taken some measures and will take some more. According to him,

> It is only one of the various steps, not the only one, and it is not meant to resolve all 'black' problems under the sun. The stock of 'black' wealth is not merely in the form of cash. It can be in the form of gold, real estate and other properties. That kind of non-cash 'black' will also be addressed through other measures.

Modi in his address to the nation on 8th November 2016, said, "there comes a time in the history of a country's development when a need is felt for a strong and decisive step." He propounded two primary reasons for this decision one was to "check enemy from across border...using fake currency notes" and the other was to "break the grip of corruption and black money".

The former Prime Minister Manmohan Singh (ch.2) though is supportive of the sentiment behind this mammoth decision, is sceptical about its execution. He says, "Both these intentions are honourable and deserve to be supported whole-heartedly. Counterfeit currency and black money are as grave a threat to the idea of India as terrorism and social division. They deserve to be extinguished using all the firepower at our disposal".

He is, however, of the view that the underlying premise behind the decision of the Prime Minister to render ₹500 and ₹1,000 currencies as illegal overnight seems to be this false notion that 'all cash is black money and all black money is in cash'. This is far from reality. In conclusion he remarks,

> Black money is a menace to our society that we need to eliminate. In doing so, we have to be mindful of the potential impact on hundreds of millions of other honest citizens. ....Leaders and governments have to care for their weak and at no point can they abdicate this responsibility... Waging a war on black money may sound enticing. But it cannot entail even a single loss of life of an honest Indian.

Calling demonetisation as the most drastic measure ever taken in India to unearth black money, Nitin Desai (ch.3) states, "this attack on illegal transactions has inconvenienced legitimate transactions at a scale which, perhaps, was not anticipated. Demonetising these notes amounts to a drastic 86 per cent reduction in money supply for the enterprises and households who work largely on a cash basis".

Ajay Shah (ch.4) argues that if a significant scale of firm failures were to come about as a result of demonetisation of 86 per cent of total volume of cash, it would convert a temporary shock into a deeper, a more long term recession.

Suyash Rai (ch.5) starting with the original objectives of November 8 announcement of demonetisation and how the new objectives were tacked on, turning India into a cashless economy states that a cost benefit analysis suggest that benefits from demonetisation were relatively small compared with the costs. Concluding his detailed analysis of the expected impact of demonetisation on: fake currency, black money, poor, rights of individual citizens, rule of law, society and institutions, he states that the original assumptions underlying the decision remain unclear, but it seems to be causing considerable harm.

> All this harm is likely to buy us only small dent on the black money problem and the elimination of a few hundred crores of fake currency. This is not a good bargain, specially considering the long term consequences.

The next two chapters (ch.6 and ch.7) look in to the impact of demonetisation on economic growth. Radhika Pandey and Rajeswari Sengupta (ch.6) state that in "most emerging economies, an important driver of GDP (gross domestic product) growth is investment demand. In India, private sector investment has been sluggish for consecutive quarters over the last two years. The principal driver of GDP growth in India in recent times has been private consumption demand, which contributes 60 per cent to the GDP".

The announcement by the government to ban the ₹1,000 and ₹500 currency notes is a monetary contraction that will translate into a massive negative shock for consumption demand. As more and more firms start feeling the pressure of declining demand, investment will get adversely affected. The combination of a slowdown in consumption and investment may result in a fall in GDP growth rate lasting beyond two quarters. The longer the time taken to normalise the situation the deeper will be damage inflicted upon the real economy and some of the damage caused may end up being irreversible. Perhaps a year later, it would be worthwhile to ask whether the cost in terms of protracted economic slowdown were worth the benefits arising from the move, remark Radhika and Rajeswari.

Chapter 7 by C.S.C. Sekhar takes up the issue of the Demonetisation and Indian Agriculture. After posing the questions what are the implication of demonetisation for agriculture, is the growth going to be severely dented, are farmers going to be in distress, which crops and operation are going to be worst hit, he states since most of the agricultural transactions are carried out using cash, demonetisation is bound to affect agriculture relatively more in the short to medium term. However, the effect varies depending upon the stage of production and types of operations involved at that stage. Primarily the effect is expected to be on *rabi* production, *kharif* marketing and prices.

According to Sekhar agri-growth in 2016-17 may not deviate from the forecast because of the way in which income in the agricultural sector in computed. However, the increased production and the expected higher growth are unlikely to translate into improvement in farmers' incomes. Paradoxically, the increase in production resulted in a worsening of farmers' situation. The large increase in production resulted in a sharp drop in prices and the public procurement of crops like pulses was not active enough. Even market transactions were sluggish after the demonetisation. There are reports of a steep decline in transactions at various states' APMCs, in some cases declining up to 70 per cent, in the aftermath of demonetisation. Thus, demonetisation is unlikely to effect agricultural growth but it is likely to hit farmers badly unless the public procurement of pulses improves and distress sale of perishable are addressed.

Demonetisation was a large adverse shock. On what horizons will the demonetisation shock play out? Now that the currency notes have come back into the economy, the interesting question is: will the recovery be quick or slow? According to Ajay Shah a slow recovery is likely (ch.8).

After analysing the various shocks to the economy: the monetary shock, shocks to exports, shocks to investments, shocks to banking and shocks to demand, Ajay Shah states,

> The key intuition of macroeconomics is about many moving parts, all of which feed into each other. Banks crimp lending, which affects demand. More uncertainty and reduced margins make firms invest less, which hurts demand. Less cash gives less buying, which hurts demand. Inventories pile up, and then firms cut back on production. This means buying fewer raw materials and labour. The workers who are laid off buy less, and that exacerbates the problem. This is the process that will play out in calendar 2017.

But then there are deeper disruptions which will have a more sustained adverse impact on GDP beyond 2017. The common perception is that once cash is back to normal levels e.g. May 2017 life will return to normal. Macroeconomies do not work like that.

Parthasarathi Shome (ch.9) remarks, "policymakers would realise that not just tax evaders, smuggler or terrorists use cash but also the poor. The leaders of democracy have not been observed to queue at banks like the urban commoner. Thus, it is ironic for political representatives to proclaim that the entire country is with them... Whatever occurs ahead, a monitoring cell should be established to minimise adversity, reflecting its gravity, for honest taxpayers and the vulnerable".

According to Mihir Sharma (ch.10) demonetisation can not be defended as a good idea, poorly implemented. The first rule of governing India is that you only make policies, you can implement. If you ignore implementation then no doubt, the License Raj was a brilliant idea too. While the government views demonetisation as a big bang reforms "its implications show that far from being an efficient manager, Mr Modi fails comprehensively when it comes to thinking at a scale...and its conception demonstrate that this government is simply amateurish in terms of economic policymaking to properly address India's deep problems".

The crisis on account of demonetisation according to Ajay Shah (ch.11) has come in a particularly difficult global context. China, Europe and the US are in great stress and impending economic distress which will harm the prospects for Indian economic recovery by giving us weak external demand. A buoyant world economy has helped power Indian business cycle recoveries in the past. This is unlikely in 2017. Business cycle recoveries in India are about surges in export demand and investment demand. We do not know how bad the demonetisation recoveries will be but the timing for this was particularly unfortunate given that one of the two pathways for recovery faces difficulties.

Ila Patnaik (ch.12) is of the view that demonetisation and its handling has undermined the public's confidence in the Reserve Bank's capabilities and its commitment to the inflation target. To overcome the shortage of cash, government and the RBI have appealed to the public to adopt electronic payments. It increasingly appears as if that, rather than black money held in cash, was the main objective of demonetisation. If we are moving towards the goal of cashlessness, government's next steps should be focused on technology, appropriate competitive regulatory framework and consumer protection. Permanent adoption of electronic payment systems will depend on the ease of payments and the charges to be paid for these services.

The next 2 chapters (ch.13 by T.C.A. Srinivasa-Raghavan and ch.14 by S.L. Rao) highlight the debate on black money. TCA talks about three shades of black. According to him what everyone has overlooked is that in the nicer democracies there are only two types of black money. One is the hidden income of honest people. Another is the income—necessarily hidden—of criminals. But India has a third type, and it is a "type"—or "class"—because of the large numbers involved of both persons and amounts. This is the income earned by the agents of the sovereign who earn via simple extortion to do what they are paid to do. Indeed, India is possibly the only country in the world where the employees of the sovereign extort each other as well. They spare no one, not even the dead at the cremation ground where they demand a bribe for dry wood. That is why, if he wants to succeed fully, Mr Modi must go after this lot first, instead of allowing them to harass the generally honest income earners.

According to S.L. Rao (ch. 14) black money has not paid taxes and does not feature in the national and tax accounts. While it is held as cash, it is also in *benami* bank accounts, converted into undeclared gold and jewellery, in real estate, and is also moved abroad and held there in bank accounts or as investments. Eliminating it requires rigorous investigation and honest prosecution. Both have been infrequent.

To minimise corruption, our administrative systems need to be revamped. Responsibility for actions and decisions must be attributed to individuals and not groups. Penalties for those caught must be made really severe. The belief that devaluing to zero of ₹500 and ₹1000 notes would soon eliminate black money and dent corruption is not merely optimistic but is also ignorant. There are many major actions that are needed before we can get there. Demonetisation is a small step, poorly thought through and implemented.

Rajiv Kumar (ch.15) has emphatically stated that for demonetisation to work, Modi must root out political and bureaucratic corruption. The government has to ensure and assure the people that they will not be hounded and terrorised by the income tax bureaucracy that may see itself as having been doubly empowered. Simultaneously, measures will have to be initiated to roll back political corruption that generates black money. Without these follow-up measures, a great opportunity would have been wasted. It would then be difficult for Modi to counter the charge, currently being hurled at him by those who oppose this move, that demonetisation with all its attendant pains and disruptions was not undertaken for serving national interest but instead to serve some narrower political and personal agenda.

According to Nitin Desai (ch.16) the massive demonetisation exercise undertaken by the government which has caused widespread disruption of cash transactions must be used to secure longer term policy and institutional changes that constrain sufficiently the reemergence of these malpractices. One such area is the financing of elections by candidates and political parties. Public funding of candidates or parties requires a more credible law on spending and a much tougher monitoring process than at present. It has to go hand in hand with a radical reforms in the functioning of political parties. Public funds should only go to parties that meet certain mandatory standards of inner party democracy and transparency in their income and expenditure. Putting an end to political corruption will be a game changer for our democracy and law and order as it will break the politician criminal nexus.

According to Govinda Rao (ch.17) if the government is serious about tackling the menace of black money it should begin with cleaning political funding. The high moral ground taken by the prime minister will be amply justified if the ruling party throws open its books of accounts to independent audit and subject itself to the Right to Information Act.

Chapter 18 by Y.K. Alagh provides an historical account of demonetisation and its impact in the year 2017. The economy has gone through a major upheaval. The most important issue and the first action point now is restoration of faith in currency rather than instil fears.

Praveen Chakravarty (ch.19) has demonstrated the changing narrative of demonetisation. He has shown, how between 8 November and 27 November, the objective for the demonetisation exercise has swung from black money elimination to going cashless. Either the Prime Minister has realised that the original primary objective of eliminating black money may not be met or there was not adequate thought behind the decision. Either way, it is worrisome.

Urging citizens to use less cash and resort to digital transactions is a laudable objective and must certainly be encouraged. But when a decision to remove a whopping 86 per cent of the country's currency is taken overnight with all its attendant costs, there has to be one strong rationale for it, even if it meant achieving multiple objectives.

The last chapter (ch.20) by Radhika Pandey and Bhargavi Zaveri raises legal questions about demonetisation. The present legal framework is unclear on the adequacy of reserves of RBI. While this has led to widespread speculation on what will happen to any windfall that may be realised from the demonetisation event, the issue of distribution of surplus by RBI is not a one time problem. This problem will continue to crop up every time RBI has surplus profits. To ensure transparency in the distribution of surplus from the central bank to the CFI and to ensure the independence of the central bank in making such decisions, revisiting the legal framework governing reserves and the surplus distribution policy is imperative.

In conclusion, I would like to reiterate that in a country like India where corruption is all pervasive, fighting black money and its continuous generation should be a major task for any government. Widespread corruption not only harasses the common man at every step, it is a deterrent to the development of the economy and the society. It is now becoming clear that demonetisation, the way it has been implemented, will not eliminate existing black money and corruption.

The worsening situation of the masses in rural and urban areas has been extensively reported in the media—not only the wage-earning poor but the middle class too are adversely affected. Millions of working hours have been lost by standing in long queues. The country is being driven into an artificially created recession and the level of economic activity is declining. According to some estimates India's growth could slip to as low as 3.5 per cent as a result of demonetisation compared to earlier projections of 6.8 per cent (*The Hindu*, 19 November 2016). The revival of the economy will no doubt be a painful process, but the sooner we have a road map, the better off we will be.

1

BIBEK DEBROY

Demonetisation Demythified

WE need to dispose of some preliminaries first. 'Demonetisation' means that some kind of currency unit loses its status as legal tender. This is different from a currency being withdrawn from circulation. A currency unit may be withdrawn from circulation, but can continue to remain legal tender. In America, Section 102 of the US Coinage Act of 1965 is a guarantee against any future demonetisation.

> All coins and currencies of the United States (including Federal Reserve notes and circulating notes of Federal Reserve banks and national banking associations), regardless of when coined or issued, shall be legal tender for all debts, public and private, public charges, taxes, duties, and dues.

It is important to make this point, since there are misinformed reports that the US 'demonetised' high-denomination notes in 1969. What was done was withdrawal from circulation, not demonetisation. The European Central Bank's (ECB's) decision on the €500 note is no different.

In the Indian case, there is legislation that allows for demonetisation. This is the High Denomination Bank Notes (Demonetisation) Act of 1978, passed in March that year, and originally enacted as an ordinance. Its Preamble indicates that it was enacted to address the issue of illicit money transfers.

> An Act to provide in the public interest for the demonetisation of certain high denomination bank notes and for matters connected therewith or incidental thereto. Whereas the availability of high denomination bank notes facilitates the illicit transfer of money for financing transactions which are harmful to the national economy or which are for illegal purposes and it is therefore necessary in the public interest to demonetise high denomination bank notes.

High-denomination here means 'a bank note of the denominational value of one thousand rupees, five thousand rupees or ten thousand rupees'. Among other things, this statute prescribes a process for an individual or enterprise to surrender such bank notes to a bank. One should note that when the equivalent amount is paid to the holder in some other currency unit, this is not necessarily paid into a bank account, not under the 1978 statute. If the individual or enterprise does not have a bank account, once identity has been established, the amount can also be paid in cash.

But this doesn't mean that demonetisation has to be necessarily done through an ordinance or statute. Consider the Reserve Bank of India (RBI) Act, 1934. Section 24(2) states:

> The Central Government may, on the recommendation of the Central Board, direct the non-issue or the discontinuance of issue of bank notes of such denominational values as it may specify in this behalf.

Section 26(2) adds:

> On recommendation of the Central Board the Central Government may, by notification in the Gazette of India, declare that, with effect from such date as may be specified in the notification, any series of bank notes of any denomination shall cease to be legal tender save at such office or agency of the Bank and to such extent as may be specified in the notification.

Does this cover demonetisation or withdrawal of notes from circulation? Despite the extensive media coverage of demonetisation, I don't think too many people have focused on this, a difference that is more than pedantic. I don't know the answer. It can only be interpreted judicially or legally. After ₹500 and ₹1,000 notes have been withdrawn from circulation from the midnight of 8th November, would the RBI—not banks, mind you—still have to redeem them at face value at whatever future date, even beyond 30th December 2016?

In 2015, the Institute for Business in the Global Context brought out a study titled, "The Cost of Cash in India". This mentions that in 2012, 87 per cent of transactions in India were cash-based, even though the share of non-cash transactions has been increasing.

> India's cash intensity also stands out in contrast to other developing countries. The value of notes and coins in circulation as a percentage

> of GDP in India is 12.04 per cent, compared to 3.93 per cent in Brazil, 5.32 per cent in Mexico, and 3.72 per cent in South Africa.

This study also highlights behavioural patterns that drive the demand for cash:

> Most consumers see three main benefits of cash. Cash confers power on buyers, since they can offer fixed bids for a bundle of goods and services... Two-thirds of the respondents appreciate that cash assures exact payment... We also find that cash-only consumers know far less about credit cards.

There are costs, as well as perceived benefits, associated with holding cash. Section 40A(3) of the Income Tax Act recognises this, since it disallows deductions on expenditure made in cash but only if the payment is more than ₹20,000 per day. While a switch to non-cash payments is desirable and there can be incentives to encourage electronic payments, cash payments will not disappear instantaneously. Having said this, one must be careful in hastily citing lack of financial inclusion. As of 9 November 2016, 255.1 million Pradhan Mantri Jan Dhan Yojana (PMJDY) accounts have been opened, 156.7 million in rural India. Also, 194.4 million Rupay cards have been issued. I am not discounting the problem of financial inclusion. However, with rapid changes, many more people now have bank accounts, even among the poor. It is a different matter that they don't necessarily use those accounts, or know that debit cards can be used for transactions and not just for ATM withdrawals. Reactions like, "My maid doesn't have a bank account, my driver doesn't have a bank account" are probably exaggerated.

There is indeed a correlation between the use of cash and the size of the informal economy. The unorganised sector can be estimated either as a share of employment or as a share of GDP.

Either way, its proportion in India is large. A 2012 Report of the National Statistical Commission on this sector stated,

> More than 90 per cent of the workforce and about 50 per cent of the national product are accounted for by the informal economy.

Most estimates that float around of the black economy's share in GDP are actually estimates of the size of the informal economy in GDP, and this vital distinction is missed. Any notion of 'black' must have an element of illegality associated with it. This is made abundantly clear in a 2012 White Paper brought out by the Ministry of Finance on black money:

> Black money is a term used in common parlance to refer to money that is not fully legitimate in the hands of the owner. This could be for two possible reasons. The first is that the money may have been generated through illegitimate activities not permissible under the law, like crime, drug trade, terrorism, and corruption, all of which are punishable under the legal framework of the state. The second and perhaps more likely reason is that the wealth may have been generated and accumulated by failing to pay the dues to the public exchequer in one form or other. In this case, the activities undertaken by the perpetrator could be legitimate and otherwise permissible under the law of the land but s/he has failed to report the income so generated, comply with the tax requirements, or pay the dues to the public exchequer, leading to the generation of this wealth.

I will call the first, where the activity itself is illegal, double black. I will call the second, where the activity isn't illegal, but taxes haven't been paid, single black. A black economy has elements of both.

In 1978, notes of ₹1,000, ₹5,000 and ₹10,000 were demonetised. What was high-denomination in 1946 or 1978 is not necessarily so in 2016, because inflation erodes the currency's value

The White Paper also made other important points. First, the dividing line between white and black is not cast in stone. One blurs into the other. Second, there is a difference between the stock of black wealth and the creation of future black income. While a lot of attention focuses on the former, the latter is just as important, if not more. The last proper estimate of the black economy in GDP, and not the informal economy in GDP, goes back to the mid-1980s. That study by the National Institute of Public Finance and Policy (NIPFP) got a figure of around 20 per cent of GDP, far lower than the 40 per cent figure that floats around. Because of various measures, the figure today is bound to be lower than 20 per cent. The White Paper identified specific areas for reforms—taxes, the financial sector, real estate, bullion, jewellery, mining, equity trading, the cooperative sector and elections.

In 2014, the RBI withdrew some notes—on which the date of printing was not printed—from circulation. However, this wasn't demonetisation. The first such exercise was done in January 1946, when currency notes with denominations higher than ₹500 were demonetised. The ostensible reason then was the same as in 1978, the curbing of illicit transactions. Since high-denomination notes (of ₹1,000, ₹5,000 and ₹10,000) were reintroduced in 1954, eight years later, one deduces that this 1946 experiment wasn't terribly successful. It is sometimes suggested that the 1971 Direct Taxes Enquiry Committee (aka the Wanchoo Committee) recommended demonetisation. Its final report had nothing to say on this matter, although it did endorse the views stated in the Committee's interim report of 1970. This report had a somewhat inconsistent view on demonetisation. It accepted that the 1946 exercise didn't work. "Demonetisation was not successful then, because only a very small proportion of total notes in circulation were demonetised in 1946 and its worth was ₹1,235.93 crore," it said and then went on to recommend demonetisation.

Madhav Godbole, in his book *Unfinished Innings: Recollections and Reflections of a Civil Servant* (Orient Longman, 1996), has the following to say about what happened thereafter:

> In the middle of 1971 the Direct Taxes Enquiry Committee, popularly known as the Wanchoo Committee, submitted an interim report in which, inter alia, it recommended the demonetization of high-value currency notes. As soon as the report was received, it was discussed in a series of meetings in the Finance Minister's room. By that time Y.B. Chavan had been shifted as Finance Minister. After detailed consideration, it was decided to undertake a series of steps, including demonetisation, as recommended by the committee. In view of the sensitive nature of the subject and the need for maintaining utmost secrecy, it was decided that the Finance Minister should speak to the Prime Minister and obtain her approval to the proposed course of action before further steps were initiated. Accordingly the Finance Minister spoke to the Prime Minister. As he told me on his return from the meeting, the conversation was very brief and very crisp. When Y.B. Chavan told her about the proposal for demonetisation and his view that it should be accepted and implemented forthwith,

> she asked Chavan only one question: "Chavanji, are no more elections to be fought by the Congress Party?" Chavan got the message and the recommendation was shelved.

In other words, anything like demonetisation requires political courage and conviction.

Later, in 1978, notes of ₹1,000, ₹5,000 and ₹10,000 were demonetised. What was high-denomination in 1946 or 1978 is not necessarily so in 2016, because inflation erodes the currency's value. Consequently, the ₹500 note was re-introduced in 1987 and the ₹1,000 note in 2001. How many notes were surrendered in 1978? They amounted to around 1 per cent of the total circulation of notes then. A different figure is more pertinent. At that time, the total value of high-denomination notes was ₹146 crore. Of this, ₹125 crore was surrendered to the RBI—that is, 85 per cent. We simply don't know what happened to the remaining ₹21 crore. Somewhat speculatively, we can state the following: For 15 per cent of those notes' holders, their stock of black wealth was destroyed, but in the process, 85 per cent of their holders were put through some inconvenience.

The NIPFP study mentioned earlier also had specific comments on the 1978 effort.

> The government has resorted to demonetisation of high-denomination currency notes on two occasions, once in 1946 and again in 1978. A crude index of the penal success of this measure is given by the value of high denomination notes which were not presented for conversion. By this yardstick, neither venture was a success. In 1946 only about ₹9 crore of high denomination notes, out of a stock of ₹144 crore in circulation, were presented for conversion. In 1978 the value of unconverted high denomination notes was ₹20 crore out of a circulation of ₹145 crore (note that the figures were actually ₹21 crore and ₹146 crore). Quite apart from the relatively paltry results obtained on the two occasions on which it has been tried, there are other good reasons to doubt the efficacy of this measure in combating black income generation. First, the measure is limited to inflicting penalties on those who hold their black wealth in the form of cash at the moment of demonetisation. There is every reason to believe that cash is not an important form for holding black wealth... especially for those who are active participants in black

> income generation. So the distribution of the penalty is likely to have little correlation with the distribution of black wealth. Second, even for holders of cash, there exist avenues for converting high denomination notes into lower valued ones, at a discount, through intermediaries. Third, and perhaps most importantly, the measure does not address the underlying causes of black income generation. Hence, subsequent generation of such incomes can continue unabated with due precautions for the form in which unspent black incomes are held. The once- and-for-all penalty exacted by demonetisation simply puts everyone on their guard for the future, but does nothing to alter the incentives which spawn the black incomes. Of course, since cash is the principal vehicle for conducting black transactions, there is undoubtedly a temporary dislocation in such activities. The point is that the dislocation is temporary.

Many people who criticise the present demonetisation do not realise that we have been down this route before and every argument being made today has been made earlier.

At the end of March 2016, the banknotes in circulation were worth ₹16 lakh crore. A little over ₹6 lakh crore was in the form of ₹1,000 notes and almost ₹8 lakh crore was in the form of ₹500 notes. There has been a disproportionately high increase in cash holdings with the public, and much of that is in the form of these denominations. We don't quite know why either has happened. The electoral cycle—including state elections—is not a convincing answer, since this cycle is almost a continuous one. It may well have something to do with the fact that both real estate and capital markets are down and therefore more cash is being held. Of course, the ₹1,000 note that has just been phased out didn't exist before 2001, so its share before that was non-existent. On the demand side, the increase in its usage isn't unusual, considering the inflation since. But there is a supply side, too. In absolute terms, a higher denomination note may cost more to print, but in relative terms it's cheaper. On an average, a smaller note also lasts for a shorter period. The smallest lasts for about a year, ₹100 for around 3-4 years and ₹500 or ₹1,000 note for 5-7 years. Therefore, there are significant costs associated with moving all transactions to low-denomination notes.

Fake Indian currency notes deserve a mention. During 2015-16, by RBI-published data, 632,926 pieces of fake currency notes were detected. (The share in circulation is a function of whether one counts the number of pieces or value.) Single-shot demonetisation doesn't solve the problem of fake and counterfeit notes in perpetuity. As in other forms of crime, this activity could go on. Technology enables better security features, but criminals also get better at it after some time. Surely, not being able to close the loop eternally isn't a plausible argument for taking no action against fake currency. Here is a quote from a Finance Ministry press release on 8 November 2016:

> Fake Indian Currency Notes (FICN) in circulation in these denominations are...larger as compared to those in other denominations. For a common person, the fake notes look similar to genuine notes. Use of FICN facilitates financing of terrorism and drug trafficking. Use of high denomination notes for storage of unaccounted wealth has been evident from cash recoveries made by law enforcement agencies from time to time. High denomination notes are known to facilitate generation of black money. In this connection, it may be noted that while the total number of bank notes in circulation rose by 40 per cent between 2011 and 2016, the increase in number of notes of ₹500/- denomination was 76 per cent and for ₹1,000/- denomination was 109 per cent during this period. New Series bank notes of ₹500/- and ₹2,000/- denominations will be introduced for circulation from 10th November, 2016. Infusion of ₹2,000/- bank notes will be monitored and regulated by RBI. Introduction of new series of banknotes which will be distinctly different from the current ones in terms of look, design, size and colour has been planned.

The demonetisation of 8th November isn't meant to address creation of new 'black' income. For that, the Government has already taken some measures and will take some more. On steps that have already been taken, the Finance Ministry press release has a listing:

> In the last two years, the Government has taken a number of steps to curb the menace of black money in the economy including setting up of a Special Investigation Team (SIT); enacting a law regarding undisclosed foreign income and assets; amending the Double Taxation Avoidance Agreement between India and Mauritius and

> India and Cyprus; reaching an understanding with Switzerland for getting information on Bank accounts held by Indians with HSBC; encouraging the use of non-cash and digital payments; amending the Benami Transactions Act; and implementing the Income Declaration Scheme 2016.

In the world of Physics, there is no unified field theory. I wonder why people look for one when the question of black income arises. The Government didn't claim that. The action of 8th November was meant to address the present stock of it, not its fresh creation.

It is only one of various steps, not the only one, and it isn't meant to resolve all 'black' problems under the sun. The stock of 'black' wealth isn't necessarily in the form of cash. It can be in the form of gold, real estate and other property. That kind of non-cash 'black' will also be addressed through other measures. As for the stock of 'black money' in cash that has become invalid, my guess is as good as yours. Perhaps around ₹5 lakh crore of those notes is 'black' in both the senses combined. The remaining ₹9 lakh crore is legal cash. Of this, perhaps ₹7 lakh crore is cash in active use for transactions. When notes are demonetised, this gets drawn out of the system and is replaced by new notes. Sure, this inconveniences people. But as citizens, are we prepared to tolerate this inconvenience, or are we saying we want the Government to do nothing about the ₹5 lakh crore? Action against that money is also an additional deterrent against the creation of new 'black' income.

Also, ₹2 lakh crore was with people, serving no useful purpose and not even earning a return for its holders. This sum now enters the banking system. Banks have more liquidity. The Government could obtain money through the RBI that can be used for public expenditure schemes. In that sense, there can be a transfer of wealth from the relatively rich to the relatively poor. Of the ₹5 lakh crore that is 'black', around ₹3 lakh crore is perhaps so in the sense of taxes not having been paid, while ₹2 lakh crore is double black. (Around ₹1.25 lakh crore of 'black' money had already come into the system before 8th November.) For both varieties of 'black', there are reports of the old-for-new exchange facility being misused by cash hoarders, through touts. I am told the going rate is ₹350 for every ₹1,000 tendered. Alternatively, there are reports of gold being bought at a premium. In either event, there is some destruction of value (even if not 100%) suffered by those with ill-gotten cash.

There remains the question of managing the transition. In this process, printing notes is the easier part. These wads of currency have to be taken to banks and then to ATMs. The more one prepares for such a transition, the greater the danger of its news leaking out and defeating the purpose of demonetisation. Since the Finance Ministry and RBI have tweaked the rules, the Government has been accused of not having had a plan and not being prepared. I don't quite see it in that light. Accepting feedback and modifying rules is a sign of being amenable to constructive inputs and is preferable to perverse rigidity. As of now, we are still in a period of transition, with crowds now easing off at bank branches. Calibrating ATMs will take longer. There has certainly been a short-term shock, concentrated in the third quarter of fiscal 2016-17. The gains will be in the medium term.

---

http: www.openthemagazine.com/article/essay/demonetisation-demythified. 25 November 2016.

2

MANMOHAN SINGH

Making of a Mammoth Tragedy

IT is said that "money is an idea that inspires confidence". At the stroke of the midnight hour, on 9 November 2016, the confidence of more than a billion Indians was destroyed. Prime Minister Narendra Modi had declared that more than 85 per cent of the value of money held in notes of ₹500 and ₹1,000 was worthless overnight. In one impetuous decision, the Prime Minister has shattered the faith and confidence that hundreds of millions of Indians had reposed in the Government of India to protect them and their money.

The Prime Minister in his address to the nation said, "there comes a time in the history of a country's development when a need is felt for a strong and decisive step," and propounded two primary reasons for this decision. One was to check "enemies from across the border... using fake currency notes." The other was to "break the grip of corruption and black money".

Both these intentions are honourable and deserve to be supported whole-heartedly. Counterfeit currency and black money are as grave a threat to the idea of India as terrorism and social division. They deserve to be extinguished using all the firepower at our disposal. However, the popular saying "the road to hell is paved with good intentions" serves as a useful reminder and warning in this context.

The underlying premise behind the decision of the Prime Minister to render ₹500 and ₹1,000 currencies as illegal overnight seems to be this false notion that 'all cash is black money and all black money is in cash'. This is far from reality. Let us understand why.

Life Thrown into Disarray

More than 90 per cent of India's workforce still earn their wages in cash. These consist of hundreds of millions of agriculture workers, construction workers and so on. While the number of bank branches in rural areas have nearly doubled since 2001, there are still more than 600 million Indians who live in a town or village with no bank. Cash is the bedrock of the lives of these people. Their daily subsistence depends on their cash being accepted as a medium of valid currency. They save their money in cash which, as it grows, is stored in denominations of ₹500 and ₹1,000 notes. To tarnish these as 'black money' and throw the lives of these hundreds of millions of poor people in disarray is a mammoth tragedy. The vast majority of Indians earn in cash, transact in cash and save in cash, all legitimately. It is the fundamental duty of a democratically elected government in any sovereign nation to protect the rights and livelihood of its citizens. The recent decision by the Prime Minister is a travesty of this fundamental duty.

Black money in India is a genuine concern. This is wealth that has been accumulated over years by those with unaccounted sources of income. Unlike the poor, holders of black money have access to various forms of wealth such as land, gold, foreign exchange, etc. There have been various attempts by many governments in the past decades to recover this illicit wealth through actions by the Income Tax department, the Enforcement Directorate and schemes such as Voluntary Disclosure. These measures were targeted strikes at only those suspected to be holders of such unaccounted wealth, not on all citizens. Evidence from these past attempts has shown that a large majority of this unaccounted wealth is not stored in the form of cash. All black money is not in cash, only a tiny fraction is. Against this backdrop, the decision by the Prime Minister is bound to have obverse implications by causing grievous injury to the honest Indian who earns his/her wages in cash and a mere rap on the knuckles to the dishonest black money hoarder. To make it worse, the government has actually made it easier to generate such unaccounted wealth in the future by the introduction of a ₹2,000 note. This brazen policy measure has neither tackled the stock of black money holistically nor has it stemmed the flow of it.

It is no surprise that the logistical challenge of replacing billions of old currency notes with new ones is a monumental one. It is a huge challenge in most nations, and in a country as vast and diverse as India it was bound to be doubly so. This is also one reason why most nations that have undertaken such currency swap operations have done so over a certain time period and not as a sudden overnight operation. It is heartbreaking to see and hear of millions of poor Indians standing in long lines to withdraw some money for basic sustenance. As someone who has experienced long lines for rationed food during war time, I never imagined that one day I would find my own countrymen and women waiting endlessly for rationed money. That all of this suffering is due to one hasty decision makes it even more disconcerting.

The macroeconomic impact of this decision of the government is likely to be hazardous. At a time when India's trade numbers are at multi-year lows, industrial production is shrinking and job creation is anaemic, this policy can act as a negative shock to the economy. It is indeed true that India's cash to GDP ratio is very high vis-à-vis other nations. But this is also an indicator of the Indian economy's dependence on cash. Consumer confidence is an important economic variable in a nation's growth prospects. It is now evident that this sudden overnight ban on currency has dented the confidence of hundreds of millions of Indian consumers, which can have severe economic ramifications. The scars of an overnight depletion of the honest wealth of a vast majority of Indians combined with their ordeal of rationed access to new currency will be too deep to heal quickly. This can have ripple effects on GDP growth and job creation. It is my humble opinion that we as a nation should brace ourselves for a tough period over the coming months, needlessly so.

Unintended Consequences

Black money is a menace to our society that we need to eliminate. In doing so, we have to be mindful of the potential impact on hundreds of millions of other honest citizens. It may be tempting and self-fulfilling to believe that one has all the solutions and previous governments were merely lackadaisical in their attempts to curb black money. It is not so. Leaders and governments have to care for their weak and at no point can they abdicate this responsibility.

Most policy decisions carry risks of unintended consequences. It is important to deftly balance these risks with the potential benefits of such decisions. Waging a war on black money may sound enticing. But it cannot entail even a single loss of life of an honest Indian.

The Hindu, 09 December 2016.

3

NITIN DESAI

Demonetisation

Pains or Gains?

ON 8 November 2016 the Prime Minister announced the most drastic measure ever taken in India to unearth black money when 500 and 1000 rupee notes were demonetised. In value terms, these notes together account for ₹14.2 lakh crore, which is 86.4 per cent of the total value of the currency in circulation as of 31 March 2016.

The stated purpose of this move is to penalise the holders of black money and to get at the illegal transactions like trading in drugs and contraband and financing of terrorist and insurgent activities. With the elections impending in Uttar Pradesh and Punjab, a subsidiary and unstated purpose may have been to disadvantage cash dependent political parties!

This attack on illegal transactions has inconvenienced legitimate transactions at a scale which, perhaps, was not anticipated. Demonetising these notes amounts to a drastic 86 per cent reduction in money supply for the enterprises and households who work largely on a cash basis.

In 1978 when notes above ₹1,000 were demonetised, India's per capita national income was ₹1,642 and the demonetised large denomination notes were not in common use in transactions. The current demonetisation of ₹500 and ₹1,000 notes is at a time when per capita income is around ₹93,000. A ₹500 note represents perhaps a day and a half's wages for unskilled labour in Delhi. Given the cost of food, a family of five will spend at least ₹500 for their daily needs. These notes are very much in use in transactions by all but the poorest and their sudden demonetisation was bound to lead to the upheavals and disruptions that we have seen.

Who are the people most affected by the 86 per cent reduction in money supply? They are the small producers who buy and sell with cash rather than through banking or other formal payment channels. How many of them are there? The number of operational holdings in the country is 13.8 crore (*Agricultural Census of 2010-11*). In addition there are 5.6 crore producing or service providing establishments that employ 5 workers or less (*Economic Census of 2014-15*). So the total number of cash dependent informal sector establishments is possibly around 20 crore. If each of these has about 5 family members dependent on it for their sustenance then we are looking at about 100 crore people or about 80 per cent of our population as potentially affected by the disruption of the cash economy.

How long will the pain last? That depends on the pace at which the new notes are injected into the economy. The banks and their employees are putting in a huge effort to support the massive currency exchange process. In the first four days about ₹3 lakh crore of old ₹500 and ₹1,000 bank notes were deposited in the banking system and about ₹50,000 crore was dispensed to customers by withdrawals from accounts. Assuming that around ₹10 lakh crore is the transaction requirement for these high-value notes, at the present pace, building up cash in circulation to this level will take 80 days. However the pace of injection may go up as the availability of new notes eases and the pain may be over somewhat sooner than that.

The immediate impact on the informal sectors and poor households who work with daily or weekly cash budgets is what we see on TV and the media. But the impact of the disruption of cash transactions on the economy as a whole is also important. For instance, it is said that 80 per cent of trucking transactions are cash based. A very large number of trucks are reputed to be stranded because the drivers are stuck without useable cash for the expenses they incur for petrol, food and lodging and bribes on the way. This paralysis of truck movement will impact production and prices.

The *rabi* showings are imminent and the most urgent challenge is the largely cash-based agricultural economy. From buying seeds to fertilisers and pesticides, paying wages to farm labour and selling produce, the transactions are done in cash. District cooperative banks, which are connected with millions of farmers cannot exchange old notes though they can issue new notes against deposits. There are reports of APMCs remaining shut because of the cash crunch. This, along with the paralysis of truck movement, will impact prices and consumers, short of ready cash, will be confronted by a rising demand on household budgets. If that happens the anger in the streets may well become unmanageable.

Will it bring the black economy under control? India's national income in 2015-16 was ₹134 lakh crore and the value of 500-1,000 rupee notes amounts to a little over 10 per cent of these. We will not know till 31 December how much of this stock is white and how much black. But given that 20 per cent of the stock has been deposited in the first four days one doubts if the black component of this cash stock is much more than 2-3 per cent of national income. The stock of black wealth is much larger than that and most of the unaccounted wealth is either parked in real estate or bullion in India or has been stashed away in offshore accounts. The black economy will remain with us until we tackle the roots that lie in tax evasion, political extortion and corruption.

What of the longer term impact? If the adverse impact on the informal sector and on prices is not managed it could lead to a short-term economic slowdown, or longer if the cash disruption lasts more than a few weeks. On the positive side, the continuing travails of the cash economy may expedite the spread of banking, credit cards, and electronic cash. The clean-up of the property and bullion markets, a restraint on vulgar ostentation and the disruption of criminal transactions, terrorism and insurgency will be a long-term benefit if steps are taken to prevent the revival of black transactions with the new notes. But right now the Government must focus on mitigating the pain rather than marketing the gain.

Dainik Jagran, 18 November 2016 (in Hindi).

4

AJAY SHAH

A Monetary Economics View of the Demonetisation

THE demonetised ₹1,000 and ₹500 notes were 86 per cent of the total volume of cash in India. In this article, it is argued that if a significant scale of firm failure were to come about, it would convert a temporary shock into a deeper and more long-term recession.

Cash is used in India for a large array of transactions in the informal sector and in the formal sector. Denotifying ₹1,000 and ₹500 notes was a large shock to money supply. This monetary shock is likely to have an adverse impact upon the economy. It is imperative that stable monetary conditions are rapidly restored.

There is a tiny part of India where most activities can be done cashless. The rest of India uses cash for effecting transactions. This includes some activities of the formal sector and it includes all transactions in the informal sector. Financial sector reforms have made little progress in the fields of banking and payments. As a consequence, currency notes dominate transactions. The share of electronic transactions in total transactions in India is the lowest in the world. The size of cash relative to GDP (gross domestic product) is the highest in the world.

'Money supply' is the pool of liquid assets which can be used to make payments. The de-notified notes were 86 per cent of the total volume of cash in the country. Depending on how you define money supply, on 8 November, India experienced a shock to money supply of 86 per cent or 53 per cent.

For a comparison, a famous episode where faulty monetary policy led to bad outcomes was in the US in the early 20th century. At the time, mistakes by the US Fed led to a decline in money supply of 30 per cent from 1929 to 1933. This large shock triggered off the Great Depression. By this yardstick, our money supply shock, a sudden decline of 86 per cent or 53 per cent, is a big one.

How does a shock to money supply play out? Money is the lubricant of the market economy. It is how payments are made. If we did not have money, we would be reduced to barter. It is very difficult to find the double coincidence of a baker who wants to exchange bread for shirts and the tailor who wants to exchange shirts for bread. In ordinary times, we do not notice money, because it just works. But when money is disrupted, the working of the market economy is disrupted.

As cash dominates transactions in India, the 86 per cent decline in cash adversely impacts the ability to transact. There are people in Mumbai who want to ride in taxis, and there are taxis who are keen to have customers, but the twain can often not meet as there is no currency which can be used to make the payment at the end of the ride. This adversely affects the income of the taxi driver (a demand shock), and adversely affects the mobility of the would-be customer (a productivity shock).

For many small firms, the loss of a fortnight of income is a large shock. Some firms will tide over this using equity capital and credit. But among small firms, who are more likely to use cash transactions, there is little equity capital which can be used to absorb shocks. For many people who are adversely affected by the monetary shock, there is weak access to formal finance and formal mechanisms of credit. In these turbulent times, lenders will also worry about whether the firm is sound. Some firms will have inadequate financial depth, and will fail.

The firms that fail will exert a ripple effect through reduced purchases of goods, services and labour. The firms that do not fail will also reduce their 'burn rate' to the bone, so as to survive the hard times. This gives a demand shock: a ripple effect in the economy with reduced purchases of goods, services and labour.

The shock will propagate through the economy. All firms are experiencing a reduced pace of purchases. The formal sector is not immune. As an example, the health of the informal sector matters to the firms selling two wheelers. We will see a decline in sales of two wheelers, which will then further ripple outward as reduced purchases by the makers of two wheelers.

These problems will be greater in the parts of India where there is more informality. I am able to use my debit card to buy meals at restaurants, and my Mobikwik wallet to pay for Meru rides. My ability to do this bolsters demand for restaurants and taxi drivers. But in regions with more informality, cash is the only way to effect transactions, and the monetary shock will map to big reductions in restaurant revenues. Roughly speaking, this translates to a bigger economic shock in the BIMARU (Bihar, Madhya Pradesh, Rajasthan, Uttar Pradesh) states. This shock will also propagate out into the rest of India through reduced purchases by the backward states, of goods and services from firms in the West and South.

Is this just a temporary shock? Will the economy just bounce back when monetary normalcy is restored? The key question is firm failure. All firms absorb shocks using financial depth that is obtained through credit and equity capital. When the problem persists, the shock overwhelms the financial depth. Then firms start failing. This disrupts organisational capital. Once firm failure has happened, it cannot be undone. You can turn an aquarium into fish soup, but you cannot turn fish soup back into an aquarium. Flooding the economy with money supply afterwards would not bring back those firms to life. If a significant scale of firm failure were to come about, it would convert a temporary shock into a deeper and more long-term recession.

The output of the economy is reduced in each disrupted day because production is lowered. And, there is a race between restoration of normalcy in the monetary system versus the ability of firms to survive the storm by using financial depth. To people who think about the real economy, the role of money and finance is often underrated. The arguments above show why money is a veil, but when the veil flutters, real output sputters. It is imperative that stable monetary conditions be restored with the shortest possible delay.

This article first appeard in *Business Standard: http://www.business-standard.com/article/opinion/ajay-shah-a-monetary-economics-view-of-the-demonetisation-116111300767 1.html*

Source: www.ideasfor india.in; 21 November 2016.

5

SUYASH RAI*

The Demonetisation Decision

Event, Impact, Narrative and Meaning

.... those who torment us for our own good will torment us without end for they do so with the approval of their own conscience.

— C.S. Lewis

ON 8th November, government announced the decision to discontinue the legal tender status of ₹500 and ₹1000 notes. The original objectives were stated as: eliminating fake currency; inflicting losses on those with black money; and disrupting terror and criminal activities. Later, new objectives were tacked on: enabling growth in bank credit, turning India into a cashless economy. A cost benefit analysis[1] suggests that the benefits were relatively small when compared with the costs.

Expected Impact on Fake Currency

A study by the National Investigation Agency and the Indian Statistical Institute, in 2016, estimated that fake Indian currency notes in circulation have a face value of ₹400 crore. This is an incidence of fake currency of 0.022 per cent. The scale of counterfeiting of the Indian rupee is not out of line with what is seen in other countries, and the procedures adopted worldwide to address this include investigative actions against counterfeiters, phased replacement of old series of notes with new notes that have better security features, etc. Demonetisation is generally not seen as a tool for dealing with counterfeiting. We must also not forget that the counterfeiters will

---

*: I thank Ajay Shah and Anirudh Burman for useful discussions.

1. *https://ajayshahblog.blogspot.in/2016/11/trumping-black-money.html*

now get to work on the new 500/2000 rupee notes, while India will likely never do a de-monetisation again.

Expected Impact on Unaccounted Wealth a.k.a. "Black Money"

The analysis presented in the Finance Ministry's *White Paper on Black Money*,[2] 2012, shows (on page 47) that, on an average, the amount of cash seized during raids by income tax authorities is 4.88 per cent of total undisclosed income admitted in those cases. This data is from more than 23,000 warrants executed. Even if this decision inflicted a 100 per cent loss upon holders of unaccounted cash, this would imply a loss of 4.88 per cent of their total unaccounted wealth, which is not much of a shock for those with such wealth. If, as is more likely, the demonetisation has imposed a 40 per cent loss upon holders of unaccounted wealth (who suffer a 40% discount when laundering the money), this implies a loss of about 2 per cent of unaccounted wealth.

Expected Costs

Cash is a store of value (white or black), but it is also a medium of exchange. Most people in India only transact with cash. More than 90 per cent of shops accept only cash or very short-term credit. Large number of labourers and small value suppliers are paid in cash. While these facts may change over time, they mean that this sudden ban may be leading to disruptions in consumption and production. Compared to the 10,000 yen note (USD 137 in PPP–purchasing power parity), the 1000 swiss franc note (USD 775), the USD 100 note, or the 500 Euro (USD 530) note, the ₹1000 (USD 31 in PPP) and ₹500 (USD 15.5) are practical notes that are used for transactions. Hence, demonetisation of these notes is a large adverse monetary shock,[3] perhaps the largest ever such shock in world history. The constraints of ATM recalibration and currency printing are leading to a long transition period. Even ensuring 50 per cent re-monetisation in cash form, about ₹7.5 lakh crore, appears hard by December-end. The

2. *http://finmin.nic.in/reports/whitepaper_backmoney2012.pdf*

3. *http://www.mayin.org/ajayshah/MEDIA/2016/monetary_shock.html*

Centre for Monitoring of Indian Economy (CMIE)[4] has estimated that a few elements of the first-round impact give a reduction of GDP of around ₹1.3 lakh crore; the total impact will be higher owing to the multiplier effect, the hysteresis associated with the monetary shock, the impact upon expectations, etc.

Who Bears the Costs?

While there is much talk about the GDP impact of this decision, a unique feature of this episode is that there may be considerable other costs that fall disproportionately upon the poor. The rich have access to electronic payments, employees who will stand in queues to obtain cash, and savings that are used to cope with a decline in income. The poor lack all these. If a poor person suffers an income shock, or is not able to get medical treatment, the consequences are enormous for the individual, but the GDP impact may be negligible. In terms of welfare implications, these costs matter a lot more than the impact on GDP.

Approach to Comparing Benefits and Costs

The benefits are primarily in the form of losses inflicted upon those with black money, while costs are imposed on legitimate economic and social activities. Ordinary people, going about their lives, have suddenly been asked to bear a burden associated with the project of imposing costs upon people who have unaccounted wealth. Some of the costs are incurred by poor people, whose welfare loss might be much more for a given level of Rupee cost incurred. Given this difference in the nature and incidence of benefits and costs, before comparing costs and benefits, each rupee of cost should be given a much higher weight than each rupee of benefit.

It seems that the economic costs of this decision are likely to outweigh its economic benefits. Some have compared this decision with a surgical strike, but it is more like a nuclear strike. The nuclear option has been exercised before exhausting other options. Although measures to help people disclose their undisclosed incomes have

4. *http://www.cmie.com/kommon/bin/sr.php?kall=warticle&dt=2016-11-21%2015:12:31&msec=360*

concluded, the efforts to directly or indirectly curb[5] illegality have barely begun.[6] This raises concerns about the wisdom of using this lever of demonetisation.

The mainstream media narrative around the decision is not as pessimistic as the analysis presented above. There is a disconnect between the mainstream narrative and the facts emanating from the ground [example[7]]. In this essay, I look at the discourse, analyse the arguments which are being presented, and peer into the long term consequences.

Four key arguments are being forwarded in support of the decision:

1. It is claimed that the decision is likely to have a smaller impact on the poor than what many, mostly anecdotal, reports suggest.
2. The monetary shock can be, and will be, quickly overcome by the use of monetary policy instruments to restore liquidity.
3. This decision will expedite the process of making India a "cashless economy", with benefits that will make short-term costs worthwhile.
4. Since the decision is popular, it must be good. This raises an interesting question: in a democracy, can there be a better measure of goodness of a policy than its popularity?

Small Impact on the Poor?

Two ideas have been offered in the claim that the adverse impact upon the poor will be small:

- Cash savings as predictors of impact on the poor: Estimates based on national surveys show that cash earnings of the poor are small, and they usually lack cash savings. So, it is argued, they are likely to seldom visit a bank branch or post office, and they are not particularly inconvenienced.

5. *http://www.mayin.org/ajayshah/MEDIA/2016/six_battlegrounds.html*
6. *http://www.mayin.org/ajayshah/MEDIA/2016/six_battlegrounds.html*
7. *http://www.business-standard.com/article/economy-policy/demonetisation-in-regional-press-bankers-taken-hostage-fake-currency-racket-boom-and-more-116120100422_1.html*

- Credit as a mitigant of the impact on the poor: It has been argued that since the rural economy is significantly credit-driven, the impact on rural poor will be small. If transacting parties know each other, they would be willing to extend credit, which would make short-term non-availability of cash less costly. Given the practices in rural markets, many commercial relationships are indeed credit-driven, and cash calls are only made periodically.

I fear that a broader understanding of the financial and economic lives of the poor yields an understanding of the impact of demonetisation that is quite harsh.

The financial lives of poor households are very different from those of middle class and the rich in one crucial aspect—intensity and frequency of financial transactions involving cash. The ratio of financial turnover to assets held, during a given period, is much higher for poor households. Financial turnover is the total value of all financial transactions, i.e. putting money in or pulling money out from any informal or formal financial instrument.

Think of a middle class household with one salaried person earning ₹600,000 a year, with total financial investments worth ₹10,00,000. From the bank account, money is withdrawn and spent, or drawn down through card/online payments, or transferred into an investment instrument. If this person has a credit card, each purchase on the card would create two financial transactions of equal value—drawing credit, and repaying credit. Other than this, there may not be much "push and pull" in the person's financial life; only simple drawing down or investing up. She may occasionally take loans or switch across investment instruments. Financial turnover during a year is likely to be much lower than the total value of the financial assets owned. The cash portion of the transaction value may be smaller yet.

Research on the financial lives of the poor was presented in a landmark book, *Portfolios of the Poor: How the World's Poor Live on $2 a Day*, Collins *et al.* 2009.[8] It found that the ratio of total transaction

8. *https://books.google.co.in/books?id=XZIF1gshRL0C&dq=portfolios+of+the+poor*

value to asset value for poor households is quite large. For the median rural poor household in India, financial turnover was about 33 times the year-end asset value. This shows that even though, at a given time, a poor household has only a small asset base and small savings, they are intensively transacting. They are using a range of informal (e.g. loan to or from friends) and formal instruments (e.g. microfinance loans)—to frequently put in and take out money.

Why do they do this? Most poor households have small, irregular and unpredictable incomes. This forces them to do high frequency financial transactions in order to smooth their consumption. They are transacting intensively in the process of cash-flow management, to transform irregular income flows into a stable flow of consumption from day to day. When the poor flounder in this high wire act, they may go hungry. These are not the concerns of the middle class: their income is much more stable, and they can use their savings as a buffer. I fear that much of the commentary on demonetisation lacks an appreciation of this distinction.

Here is a table, from the book, summarising a year in the financial life of a tailor's household in Eastern Uttar Pradesh.

		Start Amount	*End Amount*	*Turnover*
Assets				
Formal	Banking savings	152.72	10.46	167.36
Informal	Saved with a deposit collector	33.47	71.13	37.66
	Saved with a moneyguard	62.76	0.00	62.76
	Goods supplied on credit	9.41	16.32	18.41
	Total	258.36	97.91	286.19
Liabilities				
Informal	Wage advance	0.00	13.60	97.28
	Shop credit	20.92	39.54	207.95
	Services taken on credit	0.00	0.00	125.52
	Total	20.92	53.14	430.75
	Financial Net Worth	237.44	44.77	
	Total flows			716.94

The numbers are in USD. The total transaction value is more than 7 times the end-of-year value of assets, and about 16 times the end-of-year financial net worth. Instruments have low end-period values but are intensely transacted, as shown in the "Turnover" column. For instance, even though the credit balance is small, there is a large turnover, which means frequent repayments. This household needs to do high frequency cash-intensive transactions just to make timing of consumption match the timing of money availability.

It is wrong to think of poor households as accumulating incomes and then going to bank branch to exchange or deposit/withdraw it. Most poor households cannot afford to do that, as their savings are small. They must actively manage incomes and consumption, using high frequency financial transactions. To the extent these transactions involved ₹500 and ₹1000 notes, the demonetisation decision has temporarily restricted the ability of poor households to engage in their consumption smoothing.

The argument about credit relationships holds true for some time and for certain contexts. All poor people are consumers, and many are also producers (e.g. wage labourers, artisans, etc). Most of the credit relationships of poor households as consumers are for the short term, as evidenced by the high turnover in credit relationships. Further, as producers, their ability to work on credit is limited by their small or non-existent savings. There are about 14.5 crore casual labourers in India, who may not be able to work on credit for long. As the remonetisation is dragging on, credit relationships are coming under stress.

It is true that credit is integral to the high frequency financial transactions of the poor. This does not mean that there is depth to cope with much larger requirements of credit on a sustained basis. Lenders might sense problems of solvency, start demanding deleveraging, and choke off credit access.

These questions, about the financial activities of the poor, must be seen in the context of the large monetary shock which has become a large negative GDP shock. The poor who work as casual labourers, especially in cash-intensive businesses, may see their employment opportunities drying up. There are reports of informal labour markets failing to generate work for many labourers who rely on such markets. There is anecdotal evidence about many small and medium scale industries and construction sites temporarily closing down. Similarly, for farmers, this is the time when crop is brought to the market and new sowing is done. Although farmers with small holdings usually do not have marketable surplus, they need cash during the sowing season. Landless labourers may be affected because farmers with medium to large landholdings are not able to get cash to pay them for sowing work.

India has a shadow economy. Many poor people work in enterprises outside the official, tax-paying economy. Many of these enterprises are doing legal activities without paying taxes. So, in that sense although they are breaking tax laws, they are not criminal enterprises as such. Consider a small brick manufacturing unit that is totally outside the tax purview. The business is cash-intensive. It is doing something illegal—not paying taxes. However, it is a productive enterprise employing people. It is in the shadow economy, and must be brought into the official economy. This means that it must be made to pay taxes and penalties, but it need not be shut down. The note ban may have pushed this cash-intensive enterprise into failure. The outcome is that the production and employment are lost, and nothing accrues to the taxpayer. This is not beneficial in any way, and may be particularly harmful to poor people working in such enterprises.

The poor are also more vulnerable to frauds and swindles that are thriving in the present environment of enormous uncertainty. The unbanked are likely to be mainly the poor, and the unexpected ban on exchange of notes has created a desperate situation for them. It is easy to say that they should open bank accounts. But in the present situation of uncertainty, we are hearing reports of people resorting to desperate measures even to protect a part of their savings. There are many reports of this happening in remote areas.

India being a vast, multi-terrain country, with uneven presence of banking facilities, there are many regions with poor access to banking facilities. The transaction cost of having to make the trek to a bank branch multiple times to exchange or withdraw cash even once is quite high as percentage of a household's income. We have heard stories about people living in remote villages in hilly areas having to rely on others to get notes exchanged, and taking losses in the process. So, for a subset of the poor living in remote locations, the costs may be even larger.

It is quite likely that the costs of this decision on the poor will be significant, and some poor people might suffer disproportionally. Poor households have no black money and did nothing to deserve this.

Use of Monetary Policy Instruments to Restore Liquidity

Some commentators have argued that although the note ban has created a shock to money supply, the central bank could soon restore money supply through use of monetary policy instruments, such as open market operations, rate cuts, etc. It is argued that the Monetary Policy Committee will, in some weeks, see the adverse shock to GDP, and vote in favour of large cuts in interest rates, which will solve the problem.

However, it is important to keep in mind the distinction between India's money supply in banks and India's money supply in cash. On 8 November, there was ₹10.5 trillion of demand deposits, and over ₹96 trillion of time deposits, which are vastly greater values than the ₹14.2 trillion of 500/1000 rupee notes which was disrupted. The electronic money supply was not disrupted; it was the cash money supply that was disrupted. This matters because cash is a preferred medium of exchange ("money") for most transactions. The constraint today is the shortage of cash. To overcome the disruption, cash must be restored into the hands of people. None of the instruments of monetary policy do that. They only enhance liquidity in the banking system. Cash still needs to be printed and dispensed through bank and postal networks.

Cashless Economy

An additional objective has been appended: make India a cashless society. It reflects poorly on the government's policymaking process to add such a big objective after beginning implementation of such a momentous decision. If this was indeed an objective, much preparation should have gone in before the decision was announced. There is no evidence of such preparation.

Cash is expensive as a store of value—it gives negative returns and is amenable to loss and theft. Many households are forced to save in cash or other similar assets, because they do not have convenient and reliable access to the modern financial system. It would be beneficial for many households and enterprises to move most of their store of value to financial instruments, but only if considerable comfort around security, convenience and reliability of these instruments is created.

The evidence on superiority of electronic payments over cash as a medium of exchange is limited and context-specific. There is evidence to support making government-to-citizen payments cashless, but even there, the last mile problems of helping the recipients access and use this money has yet to be solved. Several research studies show the poor quality of the last mile banking network in India.

For transactions involving only private parties, the case for going cashless for payments depends on the context. It would be nice to have more cashlessness, but not in all situations, not for all persons, and not for all purposes. Cash has many inherent advantages, and in many contexts, cashless instruments are not superior to cash. For example, in an area with poor telecom connectivity, cash is more convenient. People should have the freedom to choose, depending on their context.

This government push to make Indians go cashless looks like a large, centrally planned effort in mission mode. This high modernist approach is ill suited for this objective. Going from cash to cashless is a vague and complex problem with unclear pathways. Storing money in financial instruments and using it to make day-to-day payments requires regular, reliable and secure access to these instruments. This is not a simple product that can be launched across the country overnight, but a sophisticated service that needs to take into account the infinite variety of needs of households and enterprises. At its core, it is a personal choice that each one should make in their own time. If this choice, and immature systems, are forced down their throats, many persons would recoil from electronic payments.

Government is inherently bad at seeing the complexity of such issues. It is likely to unleash a badly designed mission mode programme, without understanding the package of services required to actually make cashless store of value and payments work. The programme would also be hampered by the persistent capacity constraints of Government of India. When the objective is so complex, it is better for the government to be modest, and only play an enabling role.

The way most societies have gone to less-cash is through slow, careful, detailed policy work. The willingness to use coercion at an early stage of India's journey[9] is troubling. As an example, consider shops accepting card payments. There are about 1.5 crore retail shops, but only about 14.6 lakh card devices. Should more shops accept cards? No one can decide this from the vantage point of policy-making in Delhi or Mumbai. There is no ideal number of card-enabled shops. If there are impediments preventing this, government and RBI should remove those impediments. If the right conditions exist, and if both consumers and shopkeepers feel the need, this number will increase.

We in India have a relevant experience from an episode that began in mid-1990s—the dematerialisation of (demat) shares. If government had forced households to immediately turn all their share certificates to demat shares, many may have turned their backs on the share market. They enjoyed the comfort of holding those certificates, and were not sure about the new system. Since they were given a choice, over a period of time, most of them opted for demat shares. They saw the advantages, and made their choice. This happened in a context where the numbers were quite small (the number of shareholders), but it still took about 10 years. In that example, luckily, the new system worked out fine. But it could have failed to deliver. There were many risks of things going wrong. In such a situation, coercing households to switch to demat would have been unfair. The same holds true of the idea to go cashless, and at much larger scale.

An optimal shift from cash to electronic store of value and payments will happen if enabling conditions are created, within

---

9. *https://ajayshahblog.blogspot.in/2016/01/occams-razor-of-public-policy.html*

which people can make their choices. Government's primary role in this transition should be to unleash competition and innovation,[10] while addressing problems through regulations and grievance redress. Government also has a role in ensuring provision of enabling infrastructure, which includes Aadhaar, telecom network, broadband network, etc.

There is an enormous mismatch between expectation and reality on this issue. Some people seem to assume that India could quickly go cashless during this period of remonetisation of cash. This premature use of coercion, in an under-developed payments ecosystem which has suffered from major errors of policy for decades, speaks poorly of the policy process. It is problematic to cite this complex, long-term aspiration to reduce use of cash as some kind of mitigant for this sudden note ban.

Popularity of the Decision

Several opinion polls show that the decision is popular. Consider the following conversation:

Friend: I have heard that person X in my neighborhood has kept a large stash of cash. He is now running around trying to launder it. He always flaunted his ill-gotten wealth, and it is good that he is going to suffer a big loss.

Me: The data from tax raids shows that about 5 per cent of undisclosed income is kept in cash form. So, this decision will only inflict a small loss. Person X is just one person. The data I am referring to comes from thousands of tax raids. Even if person X has a large stash of cash, it may be just a small percentage of the total black money he has. It is not worth causing so much disruption to society at large, in order to cause a small loss to the unaccounted wealth.

Friend: Even if that is true, at least all these corrupt people will lose their stash of cash. It will teach them a lesson. I am willing to incur some inconvenience for this. At least someone has done something to make the corrupt pay. It will help reduce corruption. This is about the moral standards of our society.

---

10. *http://www.mayin.org/ajayshah/MEDIA/2016/digital_payments.html*

Reflecting on this exchange, I found four important differences in our perspectives.

Statistical versus Experiential Standard

Public policy professionals like me primarily rely on statistical thinking. My friend is using an experiential standard. For a person like me, the evidence drawn from statistics dominates a few human interest stories, but for many others, it is the other way around. Since black money and corruption are emotive issues that affect the general public, most people already have opinions based on personal experience or cultural impressions. It is not easy to change these opinions. My friend is open to a statistical perspective, but perhaps it would not immediately alter his view. Most of us humans are intuitive—we form an opinion quickly, and then look for reasons to support it.

We in the policy analysis world tend to forget the novelty and the limited use of the statistical perspective in society. Statistics became systematised only around the middle of the 18th century, and was introduced in education systems much later. For countless millenia, we have been forming opinions about the world based on what we perceive in our immediate surroundings. That is our natural instinct. On this particular question, given the nature of information involved (cash as percentage of unaccounted wealth), experiential knowledge of those who do not deal in black money may be off the mark. Unfortunately, the media have done a poor job of putting out relevant information. Those who support the decision and those who oppose it are disproportionately relying on anecdotal evidence. Anecdotal evidence is useful but only to understand the nuance of specific situations.

Aggregate versus Local Impact

We differ on the scale of our analysis. While I am thinking about the aggregate trade-off between benefits and costs, my friend is looking at impact on his immediate community. Since he is a middle class professional, the costs to him and his community may be small, while, in his view, the impact on person X would be quite large.

Sometimes, it is better to think local, and at other times, it is better to have a broader perspective. Corruption is an issue where thinking local might often be more reasonable, given the way it affects us, but the larger question of disrupting black money storage might be better addressed with a broader perspective.

Any Action versus Complex Policy Projects

We have different views about what has been done to solve the black money problem, and therefore our expectations from government also differ. I am used to the long time-scale over which policy projects play out. As an example, the Public Debt Management Agency has been in the making from the late 1990s, and we are still a few years away from seeing tangible results.

As a specialist, I appreciate pawn moves within a long strategy, even though the pawn moves tangibly deliver nothing in the short run. I would thus be happy if the government keeps chipping away on the battlefronts of corruption[11] in the country, and see no need of taking such a disruptive and expensive action. My friend may not see it that way. He probably mistrusts the gradual moves, as it is not clear to him whether they are parts of a sound strategy or just delaying tactics. He is happy to see decisive action because, in his view, not much has actually happened on this front. For me, the choice is between impetuous action *versus* careful work within a fully thought out strategy; he sees it as a choice between inaction and action.

Administrative Decision versus Righteous Battle

We also differ on how we perceive this decision as an instrument of change. My friend sees this as an administrative measure but he also see it as a righteous battle in the war against "the corrupt". I see it only as an administrative decision that should be evaluated in specific and measurable terms. I am analysing whether benefits are likely to outweigh the costs. My friend may agree with this analysis, but perhaps he also sees this as a moral struggle that may include some lost battles, but has a noble objective.

---

11. *http://www.mayin.org/ajayshah/MEDIA/2016/six_battlegrounds.html*

These factors help explain why we in the intellectual world are puzzled at why the demonetisation decision was taken, but many other people (including writers in the media) are quite happy with it.

While this is a description of conditions now, things will change over time and space. Many people who are not policy professionals are opposing the decision. A key assumption behind my friend's support for the decision is that person X, the "corrupt" person, is going to suffer. In a few months, many people like my friend may revisit their views, as they would see that not much changed in the life of person X. This is a dynamic situation that is unfolding in front of us, and the change in a person's opinion about the decision would depend on many factors:

- The costs and difficulties suffered by a person and his near and dear ones. It's exciting to volunteer for a noble cause for a few days, but as the costs climb up, enthusiasm may decline.
- A person's political affiliation (we believe almost anything if we belong to a team).
- Whether one thinks of this as a moral crusade, which is to be supported simply because it was launched, and not on its measurable success.
- The extent to which one considers objectives that were added as afterthoughts (e.g. making the economy cashless) to be relevant, and the extent to which these objectives are achieved.
- One's perception about government's overall success on other fronts that may rub off on this.
- The ability of the political opponents to create credible alternatives, so that there is a real incentive to apply cognitive resources in carefully forming a judgement. If there is only one game in the town, we have little incentive to judge the merits and demerits of each act carefully.

Judgement and Popularity

Should popularity matter? A crude caricature of liberal democracy is one where all decisions are made by the people. This is not how the

Republic of India, and all representative democracies, are constructed. In a representative democracy, it is incumbent upon elected leaders to hear the people's concerns, and then exercise their own judgement to choose a suitable course of action. Governments deviate from this responsibility in two ways.

1. Sometimes, governments refer even complex decisions to public opinion. Prominent recent examples include: the 2015 public referendum on the Greek debt relief package, and the Brexit decision.
2. Sometimes, governments take decisions that appear popular (read: supported by a majority of the citizens), and use popularity as the only measure of success, without asking themselves pertinent questions, such as: is the decision harmful to some citizens? Could the decision be harmful in the long run?

In a democracy, the will of the people should matter. However, the entire machinery of modern republican governance is meant to channel popular will through exercise of sound judgement. Why is this machinery required? In an essay published in 1819, Benjamin Constant presented[12] a distinction between the liberty of ancients and the liberty of moderns. For the citizens of ancient republics (e.g. classical Athens), liberty meant having a share of the sovereign authority.

This was direct democracy—citizens had to carry out many functions of government "collectively but directly". They came together in the public square to discuss and make decisions about war and peace; to form alliances with foreign governments; to vote on new laws; to pronounce judgements; to evaluate the performance of the magistrates; and so on. To do all this, citizens were expected to devote considerable time towards public and political matters, such that the individual citizens and their private concerns were less important than public concerns. Such participation was expensive. Societies had to depend on slaves to free up the time for citizens to

---

12. *http://oll.libertyfund.org/titles/constant-the-liberty-of-ancients-compared-with-that-of-moderns-1819*

perform civic duties, and the concept of private life was limited. Also, only 10-20 per cent of residents had the privilege and responsibility of being citizens.

Modern liberty as exercised in modern republics is very different. It is largely private, and it is enjoyed by everyone in the country. It is essentially about removal of obstructions and encumbrances that prevent individuals from doing what they wish to do. It is an expansion of the private sphere. This liberty is made possible because of the system of representative democracy, wherein governments are elected to govern, and citizens participate in politics mainly through the instrument of voting, and through part-time civic engagement during intra-election periods to keep a check on the government. A minuscule portion of the populace participates in politics, and an even smaller number holds office. Citizens elect; the elected govern; and the citizens hold the elected accountable for outcomes.

Government leaders and their advisors are doing policy work full-time, while ordinary citizens are living their private lives. Ordinary citizens do not have the knowledge or the time to choose the right policy, nor do they have the full information to judge the merits of a complex policy that has just been announced.

In this context, direct democracy is suitable for certain local issues where people can see the inputs and outcomes. For complex, macro issues, legislators and governments may seek public opinion (perhaps through opinion polls), but then they must exercise their own judgement. People demanded an attack on black money, but they did not demand demonetisation as the weapon of choice. When asked, people seem to be saying that they support the move, perhaps because they believe that it is worth trying, when other measures don't seem to have worked. However, leaders are in the arena and they must also hold their decisions to other measurable standards of success. Popularity does not necessarily attest to soundness of a policy. It is for the leaders to exercise judgement in devising the least expensive and most effective ways to attack generation and storage of black money.

Reckoning of costs and benefits, expressed in rupees,[13] is important. It is likely that the demonetisation decision fails this test. However, even if it did pass the test of a careful cost-benefit analysis, there are important elements of political thinking which should be brought into the policy discourse:

- Impact on rights of individual citizens.
- Impact on rule of law and uncertainty in the society.
- Impact on institutions.

Impact on Rights of Individual Citizens

One problem with a cost-benefit approach is that, unless it is done very carefully, it can justify inflicting a great deal of pain upon innocent people just so that society in the aggregate can benefit. Even when done carefully, it is still based on the utilitarian assumption that as long as a decision is beneficial in the aggregate, it can be justified. This aggregate net benefit is a necessary condition for a decision, but is it a sufficient condition?

In a totalitarian system, where individual identity is subsumed under the collective good, aggregate benefit is both a necessary and sufficient condition. However, in a democratic republic, individual rights and duties provide the foundations on which democratic self-government is established and sustained. Civil and economic rights must be preserved, even in face of aggregate societal benefits. For example, a poor person may not contribute much to the GDP, but is still a citizen who has a piece of the constituent power that established the State in the first place. Any consideration of costs and benefits must be over and above an understanding of the rights of individuals that cannot be taken away.

The decision to discontinue the ₹500 and ₹1000 notes is harmful for economic liberties of citizens. For weeks, their ability to conduct their economic lives are severely disrupted. Money is of no use if one cannot use it when one needs to. By restricting withdrawals from banks, which is a decision of questionable legality, and by limiting exchange of notes, people have been deprived of using their hard-

13. *https://ajayshahblog.blogspot.in/2016/11/trumping-black-money.html*

earned money when they need it. Because of the restrictions, some may be forced to take losses even on their hard-earned money. As my colleague Anirudh Burman[14] has argued, these are forms of expropriation. The right to property is a right under Article 300A of the Constitution of India, though it is not a Fundamental Right. However, intruding upon the property rights of citizens is bad policy, regardless of whether the Constitution of India prohibits it or not.

The decision has led to considerable problems for people who needed cash for an emergency, for a pre-planned social event, or for other legitimate purposes. This is an insulting way to treat citizens, and potentially infringes upon their other rights. Their ability to take care of their health, to move across the country, to practice their profession, etc., are affected by this abrupt decision. Many of these impacts are not fully captured in a simple cost-benefit analysis.

Impact on Rule of Law and Uncertainty in the Society

Order is our most fundamental need, and uncertainty is the enemy of order. The decision to disrupt the medium of exchange for so many people, and then implementing it in such a haphazard way, has generated enormous uncertainty. This uncertainty that has been unleashed could have unpredictable consequences, which ex-ante cost-benefit analysis cannot consider. For example, conspiracy theories and frauds are thriving due to this large scale disruption. Policy decisions should always try to minimise uncertainty, especially in decisions implemented at large scale. This decision fails this test.

Governments are expected to put in place system to reduce uncertainty, and to solve the problems that create uncertainty. For example, systemic crisis in the economy creates uncertainty. When Lehman Brothers failed and the global financial crisis began, the chief task of central government and RBI was to reduce uncertainty and maintain stability in the financial system.

One of the main ways of reducing uncertainty is to uphold the rule of law. Rule of law is a complex notion, but at it hearts are certain core principles. First, laws should be consistent with natural

14. *https://ajayshahblog.blogspot.in/2016/11/problematic-terms-in-demonetisation.html*

rights and principles of natural justice. Second, laws should be clear, predictable and widely known beforehand. Third, laws should be applied uniformly across similar situations. Fourth, due process should be followed, which means every application of law should provide the private party with information about the application of the law, the reasoning behind the application, and a mechanism for appeal.

This decision has hurt rule of law and increased uncertainty. When government repeatedly promised to allow exchange of notes till December-end, but abruptly banned such exchange, the principle of predictability was violated. This did not just surprise those with black money, but also put others in difficulty. The myriad rules and frequent changes are placing enormous cognitive load and hurting clarity of law. Harming property rights at such large scale without proper investigation, prosecution and conviction is not consistent with the due process requirement. Inflicting harm on the innocent goes against natural justice.

The expansion of discretionary powers and purview of the tax authorities is also likely to weaken the rule of law. The pronouncements from government seem to suggest that it is going to be open season for the taxman. They will have the authority to send notices and start investigations against anyone who may have deposited cash. This has subverted a basic principle of law enforcement: everybody is innocent until proven guilty. One way in which this principle is put in practice is by requiring a reasonable burden of evidence before investigation, before prosecution and, of course, before convicting someone. The suspicion underlying the note ban decision turned everybody depositing cash, which is usually a legitimate activity, into a potential suspect.

We look back with disapproval at the Licence Permit Quota Raj. Yet, sometimes we forget that the regime of innumerable, impossibly complex rules did not come up in one day. The rule books kept gathering fat over decades, before they were committed to a bonfire in early 1990s. This regular addition to rules was necessitated by a mindset of suspicion. There was an endless cat and mouse game between the State and the citizen, because the State wanted to control everything. If the present trend continues, a similar game could be afoot yet again. This time it would be about cleansing the society of all forms of corruption.

Impact on Institutions

Institutions are not just their buildings, people or statutory powers. They are ideas that exist in the minds of people. The RBI has earned its credibility over more than 80 years, maintaining an image of an independent organisation that values integrity. There are criticisms of RBI that it may have become hostage to its own success, and now stands in the way of India's progress in macroeconomics and finance.[15] However, its legitimacy and integrity have almost never been questioned. Now, the same institution has been placed in a very difficult position.

The way this decision was presented and is being implemented, there is cause to suspect that institutional distinctions were ignored, except as mere formalities. Government's messaging is not helping the matter. Some in the government are crediting its leadership for the idea, while others are saying that it was RBI's idea. Communications about all matters are centralised at Ministry of Finance, even regarding matters in RBI's jurisdiction. This episode is harmful to the efforts to portray RBI as an independent central bank. Add to all this the drama around badly printed notes, faulty drafting of notifications, and poor communications from the central bank, and we may have the beginning of the end of an institution's credibility.

Four decades later, the capitulation of the judiciary during the Emergency still looms large in our imagination of that institution's ability to protect our rights in our darkest hours. This note ban episode threatens to similarly cast a long shadow upon macroeconomic and financial policy in India. This episode indicates the limitations of legal protections such as statutory independence, job security under Article 311 of the Constitution, etc. The vaunted checks and balances appear to be inadequate. The Constitutional

15. *http://www.mayin.org/ajayshah/MEDIA/2010/rbi_75.html*

design of dividing power and vesting it in multiple institutions has been revealed to have severe limitations in practice, especially when a powerful government sets its mind to do something.

Another long-term institutional impact of this decision would be seen in the increase in the draconian powers of tax authorities. The nature of power of tax authorities is such that effectiveness can only be achieved by a complex system of accountability. Maximising revenue is not necessarily the best objective, as it may lead to abuse of power. The recent announcements seem to suggest that the tax department, especially their enforcement officials, will be given a carte blanche to go after depositors of cash. Since this is a high priority for government, they might err on the side of excess. Some may abuse their powers for personal gains. The damage to the institution would be lasting, and it might take a long time to restore a sense of balance and accountability.

Nature of the Larger Project

The decision is so astonishing that it has inspired utopian or apocalyptic pronouncements, depending on which side of the argument one is on. It has challenged our prior assumptions about the possibilities of policymaking in India. Is this the launch of a grand project? We obviously don't know, but it would help to consider the record of the individual at the centre of this decision—the PM. Based on the PM's governance record and work style, it seems he usually does not embark upon such adventurism. This decision is a break from his own record. Unlike Mao, Trotsky, Stalin, and others being invoked to explain what is going on, there was almost no foreshadowing for this decision.

The characterisations of this decision as an act of tyrannical overreach may be useful as warnings, and even understandable use of hyperbole to critique an egregious decision, but how do they fare as approximations of truth and as predictions of what is to come? Here is another way of thinking about this: could this decision be just an example of failure of the policymaking process? The following interdependent assumptions mattered the most in this decision:

- the portion of high denomination notes used for storing black money, and
- the pace of remonetisation with new notes.

If most of the notes are used to store black money, and if the remonetisation in cash could be done in a week or fortnight, the decision would appear very different, albeit there would still be strong arguments against it. The PM may have been advised that not more than, say, ₹5-6 lakh crore, will come back, and the remaining cash is all black money, which will be difficult to launder if the government places severe restrictions on exchanges and withdrawals. Perhaps the government under-estimated the role of cash as a medium of exchange, and as a store of legitimate value. They may also have over-estimated the pace at which remonetisation in cash would happen. For a few days after the announcement, government leaders did say that remonetisation would take just two to three weeks.

All these mistakes may appear implausible, but not if you consider the very small number of people involved in this decision, and the views of certain persons who claim to have advised the government. Moreover, the history of policymaking is replete with bad decisions when there was ample evidence to counsel a different course. It is quite possible that the process began with wrong assumptions, which were not corrected in time. This obviously does not absolve anyone of responsibility, as the consequences do not depend on original intent.

If the government indeed started with different assumptions, it must now be surprised by the ₹8.44 lakh crore (as on 27th November) that have already come back, and the long timelines for remonetisation in cash form (till date, only up to 18% done). So, the government is now forced to improvise. Introduction of new objectives (e.g. go cashless), reneging on important promises (e.g. note exchange), and innumerable changes in timelines and rules are signs of improvisation. It is dealing with the fog of a rapidly unfolding situation in this vast, complex land of ours.

It is difficult to do meaningful improvisation, because this policy decision does not allow for much flexibility. Since the decision is founded on suspicion, flexibility is assumed to be "misused" to launder money. The only way to really cut costs was to roll the decision back, once it became clear that benefits might be smaller and costs might be larger than expected. However, rolling back would make the government look inept. Most leaders would prefer to appear authoritarian, than to appear inept. They would rather be feared than be ridiculed. Hence, improvisation seems to be the only politically feasible option. The kinds of things being done to improvise seem to be making things worse. This is not surprising, because governments are inherently not good at processing information quickly and efficiently, especially in a rapidly evolving context.

I do not think that the government intended to cause so much harm. However, what matters now is what it does from here on. If the government indeed had different assumptions about how this will work out, it may now be pleasantly surprised that it has popular support for the decision. For now, this support is a source of power. It remains to be seen if and how this support will change over time. So, the next steps are quite uncertain. Has the government unwittingly committed itself to a high stakes utopian project to make an honest society out of us, and would therefore feel compelled to take more such "bold" steps? The grand pronouncements about high modernist fantasies such as "cashless India", and utopian ambitions such as "cultural revolution" against corruption, suggest that the government may take that road riddled with enormous risks and unclear payoffs. Or could the government somehow carefully climb down and go back to a governance that is focused on getting the basics right?

This event has also revealed a great deal about our intelligentsia, our media, and even the broader civil society. There is much to be thought and learnt from this teachable moment. The shaping of the narrative is instructive to watch. In my eyes, there is one effort that has suffered considerable damage: the effort to build a new conservative movement in India.

The spiritedness around the 2014 election presented an opportunity to lay the foundation for a different narrative of governance—one founded on more conservative principles. There is an ongoing attempt to build a community for nourishing conservative thought to take on the intellectual and institutional hegemony of the so-called "left". This effort is necessary for India's political and social discourse. The weaknesses of a countervailing intellectual force may have led to a certain stagnation in our political imagination. The possibilities of politics have not kept pace with the needs of our society.

If a conservative intellectual movement deepens its roots and informs principled conservative politics, in the resultant political churning, there is a genuine possibility of a different politics to emerge. Take the example of economic issues. On these issues, our present political discourse largely operates in a post-1991 consensus. The consensus is essentially about a gradual opening up to private capital, but with state continuing to occupy the commanding heights of the economy. It is a version of state-managed capitalism, but without a capable State. We also see failures of the State to get the basic tasks of governance right, while fighting innumerable battles for social and economic justice.

One of the reasons for the weaknesses of the Indian state is the baggage it carries from its socialist past. In terms of its mood, it is still a controlling, commanding entity. It wants to control outcomes across a wide range of domains. It suffers from a common curse of countries that were late modernisers: an overwhelming number and variety of social and economic demands are placed on it. Conservatism has its own excesses, but on many issues, it could provide an important counter-view to overcome the present stagnation. It could, among other things, help redefine the roles of the State, the market and the civil society, and the interplay between them.

The note ban decision and the narrative around it has emphasised the weakness of the Indian intelligentsia. We do not have a critical mass of people upholding values such as protection of property rights; who understand the need for limited government to protect civil society and markets; who oppose State-led utopian projects.

Utopian social engineering projects try to perfect human nature. A conservative perspective would suggest that human imperfections cannot be eliminated by diktat. The State can only mitigate the consequences of these imperfections to an extent. The efforts to overcome flaws of human nature should be in the social domain, not in the domain of State power. If the new Indian conservatives think that expanding state power to pursue their favorite social and economic objectives is a good idea, they should see that the same power would later be used for ends that they don't agree with. This is a mistake that many on the left had made. Further, if they think that property rights must be compromised at the altar of a project to reduce black money, they may be missing the woods for the trees.

Irrespective of what the original intent may have been, the note ban decision matches or surpasses the worst excesses of high modernist socialism in India. It was not a conservative move. The decision threatens to radically empower the government to harass and intimidate citizens of the country. It damages property rights.

Sadly, instead of forming the vanguard of an intellectual and social movement, too many are choosing to be Praetorian guards for political power. This is inherently bad for the long-term project, not because all compromises are bad, but because compromising core principles is potentially devastating for a movement that intends to distinguish itself in terms of its worldview.

Conclusion

The original assumptions underlying the decision remain unclear, but it seems to be causing considerable harm. All this harm is likely to buy us only a small dent on the black money problem and the elimination of a few hundred crores of fake currency. This is not a good bargain, especially considering the long-term consequences. I am not sure the government intended this bargain. Still, at the moment, the decision is popular.

Government may have painted itself into a corner of righteousness. Since, this decision seems to have struck a chord with a larger number of citizens, political ambition might tempt the government to double down on this path, and take more "shock and awe" decisions. It would take considerable statesmanship to veer away from this path of temptation fraught with enormous risks but questionable benefits.

The government would do well to reflect on the failures of the policymaking process that led to what appears to be a bad decision. If this was indeed a genuine mistake, and government's assumptions turned out to be wrong, it would be unwise to risk making more of such mistake in an impatient pursuit of lofty goals. Our government's capacity to run complex programmes is very limited, and it is best expended on higher priority problems, such as building the criminal justice system, achieving public health goals, improving learning outcomes in primary education, building a credible defence apparatus, ensuring provision of sound infrastructure, ensuring clean air and water, and so on.

Source: The Demonetisation Decision: Event, Impact, Narrative and Meaning by Suyash Rai, Ajay Shah's blog, December 2016.

URL *https://ajayshahblog.blogspot.in/2016/12/the-demonetisation-decision-event.html*

6

RADHIKA PANDEY and RAJESWARI SENGUPTA

Will Demonetisation Lead to a Protracted Economic Slowdown

IN most emerging economies, an important driver of GDP (gross domestic product) growth is investment demand. In India, private sector investment has been sluggish for consecutive quarters over the last two years. The principal driver of GDP growth in India in recent times has been private consumption demand, which contributes 60 per cent to the GDP.

The announcement by the government on 8 November to ban the ₹1,000 and ₹500 currency notes is a monetary contraction that will translate into a massive negative shock for consumption demand. As more and more firms start feeling the pressure of declining demand, investment will get adversely affected. The combination of a slowdown in consumption and investment may result in a fall in GDP growth rate lasting beyond two quarters.

GDP growth rate was estimated at 7.3 per cent in the July-September quarter of 2016-17. The marginal increase from 7.1 per cent in the April-June quarter was primarily driven by agriculture, construction, and the services sector. Ironically, these sectors are now likely to bear the brunt of the currency-ban shock. Year-on-year manufacturing growth rate has declined from 9.1 per cent in the previous quarter to 7.1 per cent. In the July-September quarter investment demand contracted by 5.6 per cent, resulting in a large negative contribution to the GDP.

In general, private sector activity in the economy has been weak in the recent quarters. The state of the economy prior to the announcement of the currency ban is essential because it highlights the structural weaknesses in the economy that may worsen as a result of this shock and aggravate the economic slowdown.

Cash in the Economy

Estimates suggest that the reduction in GDP could be somewhere between 10 to 330 basis points. Given the widespread reliance on cash, the actual impact could be bigger. The following highlight the dependence of the Indian economy on cash:

- India is amongst the most cash-intensive economies in the world with a cash-GDP ratio of 12 per cent. The same ratio in its peer economies such as Brazil and South Korea is one-third of India;
- Cash in circulation to private consumption ratio in India is 20 per cent; and
- Card transactions account for 4 per cent of the personal consumption expenditure.

In such a cash-dependent economy, all of a sudden around 86 per cent of the cash supply has been rendered useless. This has effectively imposed a tight constraint on real economic activity. This constraint will initially be felt most acutely in the cash-intensive sectors such as agriculture, construction, gems and jewellery, textile, trade, transportation, and real estate, as well as in the activities in the vast informal sector of the country.

Beyond the initial impact, the shock from demonetisation is likely to set off a domino effect that will impinge on activities far removed from the cash-intensive sectors. This impact may result in a protracted economic slowdown going beyond the current financial year.

It is likely that firms and households will innovate in an attempt to get around the cash constraint. Formal financial services will provide support to those who have access to them. Firms in the retail business that utilise the formal financial services will face a rise in demand as consumers shift from the cash economy to the digital economy. These innovations will dampen the effects of the shock to some extent, however, they cannot act as much of a cushion in an economy which is so overwhelmingly dependent on cash. So, even if the share of digital transactions doubles, it would still represent only a small portion of the transactions in the economy.

Will the Economy Rebound after a Short Period of Distress?

While some initial data has already started signalling a slowdown, experts opine that the slowdown in the next two quarters would be temporary and would be followed by a quick and strong period of rebound. They conjecture that as the expected benefits of the currency ban start kicking in and as the cash supply in the economy gets replenished, normalcy will be restored.

We, however, argue that reviving the real economy and getting it back on a high growth track could be a much more difficult and time-consuming process.

A continued shortage of cash is already forcing consumers to postpone their purchases, especially of non-essential goods and services. There have been reports of a decline in footfall in shopping malls and retail outlets have reported a sharp drop in sales over the last month.

In an environment of uncertainty, it is natural for economic agents to behave cautiously. Two kinds of currency have now emerged—cash and deposits. While people are able to convert cash into deposits, going the other way round is more difficult due to the administrative restrictions imposed by the government on withdrawals along with the unavailability of sufficient usable banknotes even a month after the demonetisation.

Given the widespread uncertainty about more restrictive withdrawal limits being imposed and about the time taken by banks and ATMs to disburse the new notes, it is likely that households will hoard whatever cash they are able to obtain instead of spending it. This tendency to build up precautionary savings could continue for a while even after the money supply is restored. This will exert an additional downward pressure on consumption demand.

The quantity theory of money states that there is a direct relationship between the quantity of money in an economy and the level of prices of goods and services sold, that is, $MV=PY$,

where M is the money supply, V is the velocity of circulation of money, P is the price level, and Y denotes output.

The currency ban has reduced the money supply drastically. As people hold back consumption and hoard cash, the velocity of circulation will fall. This means both P and Y have to decrease commensurately in order to restore equilibrium in the system. Estimates suggest that it may take six to eight months for the new currency notes to fully come back into circulation. The time taken to restore money supply may reduce the velocity of circulation for an even longer period, thereby resulting in a protracted GDP contraction.

Long-term Impact

A stable, sophisticated economy is one where economic agents are able to take risks as well as make long-term plans. This includes private businesses, financial investors and households. A major shock like the currency ban disrupts the overall stability of the economy. The continuous change of rules almost on a daily basis further adds to the uncertainty. Since 8 November, the government has changed rules related to the currency ban over 20 times and the Reserve Bank of India (RBI) has released more than 15 sets of frequently asked questions to clarify this change in rules. These actions create an environment of unpredictability and in such an environment, firms and households hold back their investment and consumption plans. This further puts a brake on real economic activity and it is likely that even after the currency notes are back in circulation, the brakes stay on or are only gradually lifted.

One segment of the real economy that could be severely hit by demonetisation is the MSME (medium, small and micro enterprises) sector. This sector plays a pivotal role in the economy, contributing about 8 per cent to the GDP, 45 per cent to the total manufacturing output, and 40 per cent to the total exports from the country. Given the reliance of the sector on cash, especially for the small and micro enterprises, and the cost of compliance with regulations in the formal sector, some of these firms may not remain viable or solvent in the changed environment.

Some of these firms that were already struggling to meet their interest payments amidst the business cycle downturn over the past few years may now tip over and become bankrupt as a result of the liquidity crunch. Once businesses start failing, valuable organisational capital gets eroded. Irrespective of how quickly money is put back into circulation again, some of these losses could be irreversible, thereby inflicting long-lasting damage on the growth of this sector.

The initial contractionary effect on the sale of goods and services will negatively impact business investment at a time when private sector investment is already sluggish.

The revival of private sector investment requires a sustained flow of credit. Bank credit to the corporate sector has remained tepid over the last few months. Analysis shows that despite banks receiving a large volume of deposits since 8 November, their ability to make fresh loans remains limited. In addition to this, if a large number of firms in the MSME sector default on their loans, this will exacerbate the existing NPA (non-performing asset) problem of the banks. This, in turn, may further affect their capacity to extend credit given their already precarious capital adequacy position. These developments coupled with the heightened macroeconomic instability triggered by the currency ban do not augur well for the private investment scenario.

Another long-term impact of the shock may result from the negative wealth effect on consumption demand. For example, the real estate sector is likely to take a severe hit due to the currency ban since a large percentage of the transactions in this sector have traditionally been cash-based. As real estate prices start falling due to the liquidity crunch, people who had invested their savings in real estate will experience wealth erosion and may cut back on future consumption plans. This is likely to impose a lingering effect on aggregate demand.

The long-lasting nature of the economic slowdown may also result from the ripple effects spreading across the entire real economy. It is well understood by now that the large informal sector accounting for 80 per cent of the country's employment and 45 per cent of the GDP will be disproportionately affected by the liquidity crunch because of its inherent dependence on cash. While the share of the informal sector is estimated at 'only' 45 per cent, this hardly means that majority of the economy will be insulated from the shock. A reason for that is that firms are interlinked in production. The production and sale of a good require a long chain of transactions, many of which involve cash.

If just one link in this chain breaks down, there will be problems. For example, one tends to imagine that exports will not be affected, because exports generally involve bank transactions and not cash. But that is only true at the final stage. At the earlier stages, cash can be quite important, for example, in the textile sector where many of the activities are carried out in small workshops and are cash-dependent. If a large number of these workshops start shutting down because of liquidity constraints and a decline in sales revenues, the entire supply chain in the textile sector will get disrupted. Even if the new notes come back into circulation in a few months' time, this kind of real economic disruption may last much longer.

All these point to the possibility that once GDP growth starts falling, it may take several quarters before the economy gets back on track again.

Conclusion

The impact of the contractionary demand shock triggered by the 8 November currency ban will gradually radiate from cash-intensive activities to virtually every sector of the economy. This will lower the GDP growth. The resurgence in growth may prove to be a challenge and may take longer than expected in an already sluggish investment scenario. Given the magnitude of the shock and the channels through which economic activity may get disrupted for close to a year, if not more, it is surprising that the RBI estimated the impact on growth to be limited and transitory as announced in its recent monetary policy review meeting.

It may be worthwhile to ask, had the currency ban announcement not been made, how would the economy have progressed? Before 8 November, India's GDP was growing roughly at 7 per cent, primarily boosted by growth in consumption expenditure. Private investment activity has been weak. Banks have been saddled with NPAs and till now no well-defined policy measure has been devised to resolve the problem and boost credit off-take in the economy. Demand for corporate credit has been stagnant for several quarters and an overleveraged corporate sector has been refraining from initiating new investment projects.

During this time, the singular objective of the government should have been to adopt structural reforms to stimulate GDP and achieve a high and sustainable growth rate. Generating jobs to absorb the demographic dividend while it lasts should have been another policy priority. Instead of prioritising these objectives, the government announced a measure that has in fact dealt a severe negative blow to the overall economy.

The associated policy uncertainty is contributing to macroeconomic instability. Arguably, this is the last thing that was needed now given the pervasive weakness in the credit and investment climate. Policymaking over the next couple of quarters is likely to get hijacked by this single event in order to ameliorate a potential economic damage. All this is very costly both in terms of the time spent and the resources used up in first delivering the shock and then in restoring normalcy.

The longer the time taken to normalise the situation, the deeper will be the damage inflicted upon the real economy, and some of the damage caused may end up being irreversible. Perhaps a year later it would be worthwhile to ask whether the costs in terms of a protracted economic slowdown were worth the benefits arising from this move.

Source: http://thewire.in/86227/demonetisation-economic-slowdown/

7

C.S.C. SEKHAR

Demonetisation and Indian Agriculture

PRIME Minister Narendra Modi announced a partial demonetisation drive on 8 November, thereby extinguishing the high denomination currency notes of ₹500 and ₹1000. This is estimated to have affected currency of value ranging between 14 to 16 lakh crores and constituting about 86 per cent of the currency in use. The drastic move was announced at a crucial stage for agricultural operations. The *kharif* harvest was about to reach the markets and the *rabi* sowing had just begun. There were genuine apprehensions about its impact on one of the largest sectors that employs about 50 per cent of the population. More so, since after two years of sluggish growth, agriculture has just made a turnaround with a growth forecast of at least 4 per cent in 2016-17, even by conservative estimates.

What are its implications for agriculture? Is the growth going to be severely dented? Are farmers going to be in distress? Which crops and operations are going to be the worst-hit? These are some of the questions that assumed significance in this context. The short answer to these questions is both no and yes. The agricultural growth is unlikely to be affected by demonetisation. However, the farmers are likely to be adversely affected, if not distressed.

Since most of the agricultural transactions are carried out using cash, the demonetisation is bound to affect agriculture relatively more in the short to medium term. However, the effect varies depending upon the stage of production and types of operations involved at that stage. Primarily the effect is expected to be on *rabi* production, *kharif* marketing and prices. Given these factors, what are the growth prospects for agriculture?

The agri-growth in 2016-17 is unlikely to deviate much from the forecasts. This is mainly because of the way income in agricultural sector is computed, wherein the production is multiplied by wholesale prices and the costs of inputs are deducted, to derive the GVA (gross value added). To this the value of irrigation services is added to compute the total income. Although the food prices have been on a downward trend lately, the quantum of production is robust enough to compensate for this. The *kharif* foodgrain production increased from 124 million tons in 2015-16 to 135 million tonnes in 2016-17—an impressive increase of 9 per cent. The increase in production of pulses is a huge 57 per cent! However, the food prices have been showing a sharp decline. The overall food inflation, based on CPI (consumer price index), has come down from 6 per cent in December 2015 to 2 per cent in November this year. The corresponding decline in case of pulses is whopping—from a high of 46 per cent to 0.2 per cent reflecting a much faster decline in the price of pulses. Despite this sharp downward movement in food prices, the overall growth in the sector is very likely to be in the range of 4.5 to 5 per cent, largely due to the large increase in *kharif* production. Also, the *rabi* production is likely to be very high because the *rabi* sowing has been very brisk so far.

Rabi sowing normally starts in the last week of October and extends till end December/mid-January. As per the estimates on 30 December, *rabi* sowing is complete on 92 per cent of the target area. The current area sown is 7 per cent more than the area sown last year around the same time. The area under wheat, pulses and oilseeds has increased by 8 per cent, 13 per cent and 11 per cent respectively. This is an impressive increase, considering that the sowing had just begun when the demonetisation drive was announced. There were apprehensions about farmers' ability to purchase seeds and other inputs and it now appears that the demonetisation has had little impact on *rabi* sowing. The informal institutional structures and the inter-linked markets in rural India, where the suppliers advance inputs on credit and also act as lenders appear to have cushioned the impact of demonetisation to a large extent. The government's initiatives such as allowing farmers to buy seeds using old notes from central and state-owned seed companies, as well as from ICAR and central varsities; instructing fertiliser companies to sell soil nutrients on credit; allowing an additional two months to repay crop loans due in November-December period have all perhaps helped this process. As a result of all these factors, the *rabi* food grain output is likely to be much higher and could be 7 per cent higher than 2015-16, if the targets are met. Therefore, the overall agricultural growth in 2016-17 could be much higher despite a slowdown in food prices.

However, the increased production and the expected higher growth are unlikely to translate into improvement in farmers' incomes. Paradoxically, the increase in production resulted in a worsening of farmers' situation. The large increase in production resulted in a sharp drop in prices and the public procurement of crops like pulses was not active enough. Even market transactions were sluggish after the demonetisation. There are reports of a steep decline in transactions at various states APMC's, in some cases declining upto 70 per cent, in the aftermath of demonetisation. Farmers faced a lot of hardship in transporting the produce to the market, since the services such as loading and unloading require labour which is cash-intensive. Decline in demand due to cash constraint has further aggravated these price declines. There have been several instances of market price falling below the MSP (minimum support price) in various parts of the country. There have been 785 and 209 such instances in case of moong and arhar respectively in the first week of December, 2016. The situation is worse for perishables like fruits and vegetables. The absence of storage and processing facilities for these commodities make these commodities highly vulnerable. The liquidity crunch has pulled down the demand, further aggravating the plight of these farmers. There are reports of price of vegetables dropping by almost 60 per cent across wholesale markets. The CPI inflation of vegetables has recorded a steep decline of 10 per cent as per the latest estimates. The cash crunch has reportedly affected onion trade, poultry sector and there are also reports of large scale distress sales by orange farmers in Vidarbha region in Maharashtra.

In conclusion, demonetisation is unlikely to affect agricultural growth but it is likely to hit the farmers badly, unless the public procurement of pulses improves and distress sales of perishables are addressed.

8

AJAY SHAH

On What Horizons will the Demonetisation Shock Play Out?

DEMONETISATION was a large adverse shock. We now have some sense of how currency notes will come back into the economy. Now the interesting question is: Will the recovery be quick or slow? A slow recovery is likely.

Let's start at the monetary shock. New notes came in at a slow pace from 9 November onwards. In some places, the old notes continued to be used in transactions. Old notes are now dwindling away; they will all be back with Reserve Bank of India (RBI) by 31 December. In late December, we have the biggest mismatch between the currency required to sustain ordinary business activities vs. the currency actually in place. Pay days in early January could be difficult days.

If the old notes are to be exactly replaced, this process runs till May 2017. The actual delay will be lower: Presses are making 2000 rupee notes, and not all the erstwhile cash in circulation was required as a medium of exchange. But the 2000 rupee notes are an inadequate medium of exchange, and the behaviour of people has changed; everyone will now hoard more cash. My guess is that December is the bottom, and normalcy on cash availability will come by end-March. The first round disruption of the economy would be for five months: November to March.

In 2008, monetary policy did well. RBI wisely ignored the exchange rate, and rapidly switched gears to cutting rates. Both elements (lower rates and weaker rupee) helped prop up the economy. In 2016 and 2017, the monetary system has been disrupted and it is hard for monetary policy to help.

The second shock is to exports. In September 2008, with the Lehman shock, seasonally adjusted ("SA") non-oil exports fell by 161 per cent annualised. This time, export demand is soft but unchanged. All that has happened is a disruption of domestic production. In November 2016, this decline was 76 per cent (annualised). This is a surprisingly large number, considering that nothing changed with export demand, and suggests a significant disruption of production.

The third shock is to investment. Demonetisation has created uncertainty because it casts a cloud on the performance of the economy in 2017 and 2018. It also suggests a new level of policy risk; we used to think Indian institutions ruled out such actions. In 2008 also, there was high uncertainty which adversely affected investment. It was the finest hour for the key persons of MoF, RBI, SEBI and PMO; their actions made Indian policy capabilities look good and created confidence. This time, policy work on an array of issues has stalled as demonetisation has absorbed the economic policy leadership.

The fourth shock is to banking. In 2008, treasury activities of banks were in a tizzy, and the first signs of the great NPA (non-performing assets) crisis became visible. The humdrum business of account opening, credit cards, home loans and financial services for SMEs (small and medium enterprises) went on all over the country without disruption. This time around, most employees of banks are absorbed in counting currency notes. For a few months, India has a sharp decline in the production of banking services. The macroeconomic downturn may worsen the corporate NPA problem, and demonetisation may directly induce defaults by individuals.

The fifth shock is to demand. Production planners in the large firms make decisions about how much to produce based on the flexibility of their production process and on forecasts of sales. On 9 November, every firm in India had to revise its forecasts for sales and then adjust its production process. A few data points are now visible about these developments.

In September 2008, the shock was on television and outside India. There was a shock to export demand. Not much happened in India. As an example, the sales of automobiles grew robustly in September

2008. The blow to sales came with a lag, from October to December 2008. These developments shaped the production planning.

This time around, there is an adverse impact on sales right away, i.e. in November 2016. This is more visible in cheaper things. Sale of two wheelers fell by 169 per cent (SA annualised) and sales of three wheelers fell by 289 per cent (SA annualised). In contrast, the sale of cars only fell by 37 per cent. Production managers are absorbed in revising forecasts about sales in coming months, and adjusting production. These adjustments tend to come with a lag because the shock was unanticipated and because the production process has limited flexibility.

This kind of shock plays out slowly. At first, all that happens is inventory adjustment. E.g. in November 2016, while the sales of cars fell by 37 per cent (SA annualised), production went up by 96 per cent (SA annualised). The production process is inflexible and inventories have risen. When inventories build up to uncomfortable levels, and the outlook for sales looks weak, production cutbacks begin. This gives reduced purchases of raw materials and labour. Consumer companies buy less of raw materials, and then raw materials companies buy less labour. Then workers buy less of consumer goods, which enlarges the shock.

The key intuition of macroeconomics is about many moving parts, all of which feed into each other. Banks crimp lending, which affects demand. More uncertainty and reduced margins make firms invest less, which hurts demand. Less cash gives less buying, which hurts demand. Inventories pile up, and then firms cut back on production. This means buying fewer raw materials and labour. The workers who are laid off buy less, and that exacerbates the problem. This is the process that will play out in calendar 2017.

In this macroeconomic trauma, some written contracts or implicit contracts will be violated. Some firms will fail. Everyone is trying to survive the storm, but some will falter. The NPA crisis will deepen. These are the deeper disruptions, which will have a more sustained adverse impact on GDP beyond 2017.

Many people feel that once cash is back to normal levels, i.e. May 2017, life will return to normal. Macroeconomies do not work like that.

Source: *On What Horizon will the Demonetisatin Shock Play Out?* by Ajay Shah, Ajay Shah's blog, 26 December 2016.

URL. *http://www.mayin.org/ajayshah/MEDIA/2016/horizons.html.*

Business Standard, 26 December 2016.

9

PARTHASARATHI SHOME

Demonetisation

An (un)Necessary Evil?

FEARS of a GDP (gross domestic product) setback from the government's demonetisation action are unfounded. At the macroeconomic level, whatever is the amount of black money coming into banks by December 31 and into the Reserve Bank of India (RBI) by March 31, would be estimated by RBI on March 31—what has come in and what has not—in comparison with the cash earlier issued by it. RBI will thus arrive at a calculation of change in its liabilities, and quantify mismatched assets and liabilities in its balance sheet. It will then return some government bonds it holds thus enabling government to increase spending and, in turn, restoring GDP to normal. Also, the view that black money holders will find refuge in gold is based on merchants assuming tax evaders' risk by accepting old ₹500 and ₹1,000 notes since, until December 31, that is legal. Unlikely again, since currently risk aversion is pervasive.

The problems lie elsewhere. First, consider why demonetisation was rendered essential. The lacklustre success of the income tax department (ITD) during previous and current governments to contain black money is one explanation. A white paper on black money listed measures they had taken to curb it. It was unconvincing since black money persisted despite those measures. Admittedly, Budget allocation to ITD's investigation function is too small compared to needs, in contrast to the Budget for fruitless routine assessment of all taxpayers, an uncorrected imbalance even after the Tax Administration Reform Commission (TARC) made its recommendations. If the recommended reallocation of staff resources were undertaken, black money could have been unearthed in a more unobtrusive, imperceptible and consistent manner.

Second, the government's Income Declaration Scheme (IDS) initially reported a base of ₹5,000 crore from undisclosed foreign accounts, followed by ₹65,250 crore of undeclared income in cash and other assets in India that was "likely to be further revised upwards". While the ₹5,000 crore base was believable, the ₹65,250 crore number requires deconstruction. It is likely to reflect to no small extent the expected outcomes of already ongoing actions of the tax or intelligence departments. After all, income tax officers are regularly carrying out investigation and search and seizure so that they continually gather information and possess expected collection estimates from such activities. Only if and when the government releases a breakup of the sources of the ₹65,250 crore could one assess the nature and reality behind it. Also, how much tax can be procedurally recovered from this tax base remains unclear.

It would be superfluous to repeat the inequity that emanates between good and bad taxpayers from repetitive tax amnesties irrespective of the government, a habitual quick fix of Indian policymakers that could only have exacerbated tax evasion behaviour over decades as is well known from international experience.

Lamentably, India continues to eschew benchmarking itself with other tax administrations or prevalent good practice elsewhere.

Third, tax avoidance—and evasion—occurs even in the organised sector through tax base depletion reflecting misapplication, misuse or illegal use of incentives and deductions, thus adding to the tax gap. The government's annual revenue loss calculation presented to Parliament in every Union Budget—we introduced this international practice in 2006—is testimony to tax base depletion. Yet this government too has done little to cut back incentives and has indeed given more of them for ever new so called leading sectors, benefitting primarily the already rich and wealthy. The Union finance minister's promise to bring down headline corporate tax rate to 25 per cent remains unfulfilled though he mentions its need occasionally.

Fourth is impact on the poor. To hear leaders opine that farmers can also put their money into banks is reminiscent of a policymaker of the previous government asserting to me that there must be a ration shop every 50 yards. The current authorities may take a few trips to India's deep interiors to view if all farmers do, or can, access banks and how far is their nearest bank; a mere statistic regarding new bank accounts is insufficient. Policymakers would realise that not just tax evaders, smugglers or terrorists use cash, but also the poor. Neither have the leaders of democracy been observed to queue at banks like the urban commoner. Thus, it is ironic for political representatives to proclaim that the entire country is with them. It reveals little reality check of the vast ocean of ordinary Indians.

Sadly, the suffering of the poor and the sick could have been averted. For such deeply cross-cutting action, the government should have had ready countermeasures to ensure the poor did not go unfed and the sick received treatment. Reports indicate that daily sellers in Kolkata's vegetable and fish markets were unable to sell since bangali babus do their shopping with ₹500 notes—understandably, given fish prices per kilo. Fish rotted. The sufferer was not the buyer but the seller whose daily earning feeds the family. Such examples abound.

Understood that the government's action had to be kept secret for effective outcome. But news flashes, for example, that ₹3 crore were deposited in old 500s and 1000s by government's political party, or its use of new 2000s, just before the demonetisation announcement, are disturbing. The government's full explanation is warranted. Indeed, the prime minister's advisers should have counselled him to leave behind a national address before being flashed on a Japanese bullet train ostensibly pursuing the luxury Mumbai-Ahmedabad bullet train project. A prior address would have been reassuring and effective rather than exhorting punishment post-event from Goa's shores. Is the team that assured him that it would be just a two-day pain being asked to resign or is absence of accountability being ignored as always?

Finally, further draconian policy could be expected to square the circle. Complementary would be reinstatement of the Bank Cash Transactions Tax that was introduced, and removed, by the previous government despite BCTT's success in diminishing fictitious long-term—therefore untaxable—capital gains by limiting the high velocity of bank transactions that illegally converted black money into white. Whatever occurs ahead, a monitoring cell should be established to minimise adversity, reflecting its gravity, for honest taxpayers and the vulnerable.

Business Standard, 15 November 2016.

10

MIHIR S. SHARMA

A Big, Destructive Bang

FINANCE Minister Arun Jaitley sounded more than a little exasperated this weekend, when he was asked—as he has been so often—about "big bang", or transformational, reform. "The last two years," said Mr Jaitley, "I was being asked where the big bang was. Now you ask if we can afford [big bangs like demonetisation]." This is, like most statements from high officials of this government, simultaneously true and false. It is true that demonetisation is a big bang—in the sense that it is accompanied by a terrific amount of noise, and nobody is sure for a while exactly what the explosion has destroyed. It is false, however, that demonetisation is any kind of transformational reform. In fact, given that it is statist in orientation, reduces choices for market participants, depends enormously on inefficient government machinery, and increases the costs of doing business for the foreseeable future, it is on pretty much every count the opposite of "reform".

Of course, you have to feel for Mr Jaitley. Who would want to be the man nominally in charge of driving the economy when your boss orders you to swerve it into a ditch of unknown depth? And when the justifications for ditch-diving that you must repeat can change weekly, even daily? (At the time of writing, the prime minister's stated justification was that it would mean beggars could go cashless. He had apparently seen a video on WhatsApp to that effect.)

It is not surprising therefore that, in the grab-bag of explanations, clarifications, attacks, and tearful moral posturing that has passed for government statements on demonetisation, Mr Jaitley would—almost by accident—seize on one of the most damaging. By indicating that the government views demonetisation as big-bang reform, the finance minister has destroyed two things. First, he has undermined what little remains of the government's reputation for policy-making. And second, he has fatally weakened any defence of its failure to reform so far.

Much of what the government has done for the economy has been very limited in scope. What has not been incremental has been imposed externally—the auctioning of natural resources was mandated by the Supreme Court, for example, and the GST was merely the culmination of a decade-long process. The argument that the government and its multitude of strenuous defenders provided for this timidity was that, in India, it is difficult to spend political capital on transformational reform. Even the most powerful politician since Indira Gandhi, we were told, would have to move slowly.

In one stroke, demonetisation has rendered that argument specious. Narendra Modi has shown that if he has chosen so far to avoid transformational economic reform, it is not because he is worried about the disruption it would cause or the political opposition it would create—no, it is because he simply is not interested in doing it. Who now can claim that privatisation of big public-sector monopolies or administrative reform or labour law reform was off the table because Mr Modi was forced towards incrementalism? If you decide to plunge the world's third-largest economy into a liquidity crisis overnight, then you cannot be described as being too cautious for shock therapy.

And as for what it reveals about the policy-making in this government—well, the less said, the better. Demonetisation cannot be defended as a good idea, poorly implemented. The first rule of governing India is that you only make the policies you can implement. If we ignore implementation, then no doubt the Licence Raj was a brilliant idea, too. No, demonetisation has to be either a good idea or a bad idea to begin with, with a clear-eyed estimation of the implementation difficulties being an integral part of the decision-making process.

And that is where the government's weaknesses have been thrown into sharp relief. Not only is this the extreme example of a general problem—that this government is absurdly top-heavy, with all major initiatives coming from the prime minister's office. But it is also emblematic of all the government's other policy-making weaknesses: A tendency to think in terms of headlines, not of effects; a pernicious distrust of expertise; and a tendency towards statism.

In many ways, Mr Modi is a prisoner of his experience in Gujarat. As chief minister there, he had India's best bureaucracy to work with; so he severely overestimates the agility and efficiency of the government system. His conception of political stumbling-blocks is also conditioned by his Gujarat experience—as we saw when the land acquisition ordinance had to be withdrawn, because he thought that taking farmers' land for companies would be as easy nationwide as it was in Gujarat. And his electorate in that trading state was relatively well-off and supremely adaptable—so he tends to bet the rest of the country can adapt as swiftly to economic changes.

But above all, what is revealed here is the limitations of a government that does not believe in thinking through its actions. There is something deeply amateurish about the planning of demonetisation, as if it was done on a BJP WhatsApp group in between furious discussions about cow slaughter. Where were the professionals? Let us dispense with the fiction that "nobody could have known" about demonetisation. As is abundantly clear now, rumours and speculation about it were rife beforehand. So little would have been lost if Mr Modi had consulted, in confidence, leading economists on the subject of adaptation costs. Who briefed him of ATM penetration? Of currency-printing timelines? Of supply chains for small and medium enterprises? Before you try something on this scale, do you not need to get the country's foremost experts into the room, and listen carefully to their warnings and advice?

I do not deny that demonetisation is currently politically popular. It may remain so—only in long-suffering India, perhaps, will already trodden-on people accept additional inconvenience if assured that everyone else is suffering too. Given that, immediate political popularity is not how this decision should be judged. Its implementation shows that, far from being an efficient manager, Mr Modi fails comprehensively when it comes to thinking at scale. Its nature proves that, far from being a reformer constrained by politics,

Mr Modi is simply a statist who thinks only in terms of politics. And its conception demonstrates that this government is simply too amateurish in terms of economic policy-making to properly address India's deep, deep problems. Politically popular or not, the reputation of this government and its leaders should not survive this disastrous experiment.

Business Standard, 04 December 2016.

11

AJAY SHAH

A Bad Time for a Crisis

WE in India are absorbed in demonetisation. This crisis has come in a particularly difficult global context. In China, Europe and the US, there is great stress and impending economic distress. This harms the prospects of an Indian economic recovery by giving us weak external demand. These difficulties have already given us a sharp downturn in goods and services exports by listed firms, where data is observed till the July-Aug-Sep 2016 quarter. A buoyant world economy has helped power Indian business cycle recoveries in the past. This is unlikely in 2017.

Figure 11.1

Seasonally Adjusted Non-Oil Goods Exports

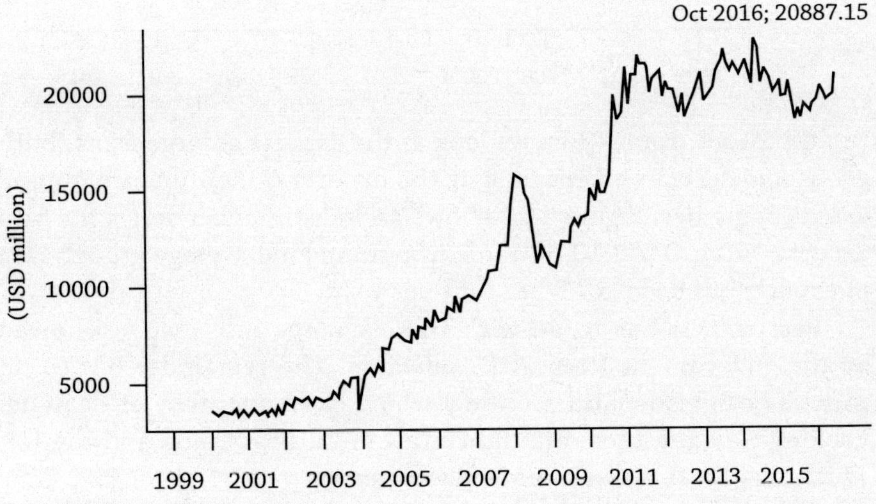

A little noticed fact about the recent years has been the problems of exports. Figure 11.1 shows the seasonally adjusted level of non-oil goods exports, measured in million dollars per month. For a long period, we had strong growth, from the region of $5 billion a month in 2002 to $20 billion a month by 2011. But after that, we've been stuck with no growth from 2011 to 2016. (This covers goods but not services exports.)

Figure 11.2

Exports of Non-Finance Non-Oil Listed Companies: Index Number Series

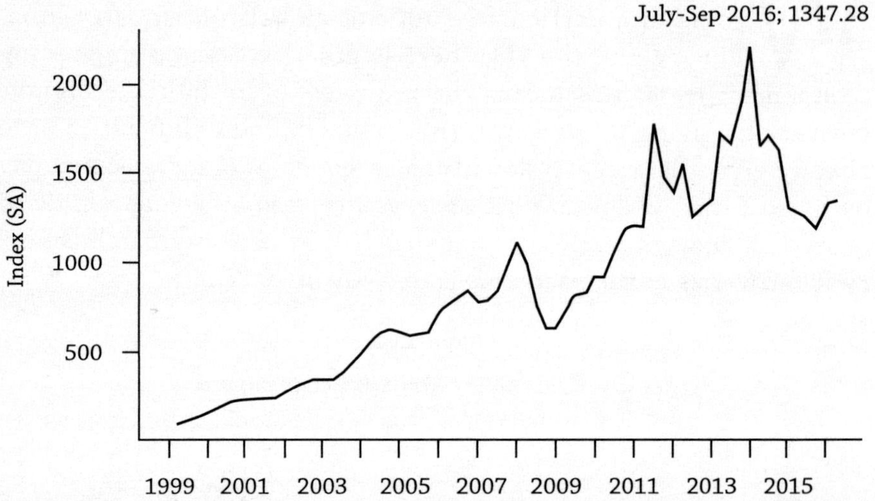

Things are worse when we look at the exports of large firms (both goods and services). Let's look at the exports of non-finance non-oil listed companies. Figure 11.2 shows an index number series for firm exports. From Q4/2013 onwards, the compound average growth rate of exports has been -17.5 per cent per year.

Part of this has to do with the exchange rate policy followed by the government from 2013 onwards. The remainder has to do with the sluggish world economy which lacks buoyancy of demand. Looking forward, there are difficulties in Europe, China and the US, which suggest that weak demand will persist.

Europe is not faring well. The Greek crisis rocked the globe. Similar problems lurk in other southern European countries like Italy. Southern Europe is trapped between two rival problems. To get back to growth, they need a substantial reduction in domestic prices and wages. This deflation would make debt servicing impossible. But if this deflation does not take place, growth is near zero, which makes debt servicing impossible.

The political capacity for thought and action on economic questions in Europe has been sapped by Brexit, the refugee crisis, and the resumption of hostilities with Russia. Liberal democracy has collapsed in the heart of Europe, in countries like Hungary. Angela Merkel (Germany) is now the most important world leader who stands up for liberal democracy, and this is a heavy burden.

Under this combination of economic and political stress, it is hard to obtain strong growth in Europe. We are likely to collapse into periodic episodes like the Greek crisis. Italian outstanding debt is roughly 10 times larger than Greek debt, so difficulties in Italy are an entirely different scale of problem when compared with Greece.

China is not faring well. The 'China model', of command and control, industrial policy, State-led development, minus civil liberties and the rule of law, did not work out. From Deng Xiaoping's time, there was a hope that China would be able to gradually evolve into a more humane political system. Under Xi Jinping's rule, these hopes have faded. China seems stuck with autocratic rule, much like the USSR and Russia. The Chinese elite is unconfident about its future in China, and is sending assets and family members out of the country.

Vast sums of money are leaving, partly out of mistrust of the China model, and partly as a speculative play on the view that the Chinese RMB will depreciate. The problem has been exacerbated by the strong dollar of recent weeks. This is shaping up as the biggest currency crisis in world history. The Chinese currency defence is now moving into the toxic phase (recall India in May 2013) where unpleasant things are done to defend the exchange rate, which damage growth.

The US is not faring well. Donald Trump is likely to bring together the least impressive cabinet that the US has seen in a century. Trump and his friends are proud of their election success, and look down upon the dorkish details of policy. But their understanding of the complexities of government is questionable. Second rate people hire third rate people, and there is the risk that the top 4,000 odd positions in the US Federal Government will add up to a weak top management team. There is the danger that major decisions will be made by a few people in secrecy, without the refinement of ideas and the project planning that takes place through the dorkish process of intellectual analysis, democratic discussion and methodical project planning.

Success in real world public policy requires a leadership that appreciates intellectual complexity, and has an emotional comfort with people who understand government. An intellectual and emotional connect with the world of ideas is required in reaching out to expertise, and in listening to them. The Trump team is emotionally distant from the experts; it is almost proud of being tone deaf on the complexities of public policy. They may resort to policy adventurism, carrying catchy slogans and half baked ideas into the domain of execution. They will then lurch from one crisis to another.

With a difficult outlook in Europe, China and the US, it is likely that global demand for exports will not help carry our burden in India. Goods and services exports by the listed companies grew by an average of 35 per cent from 1999 to 2005, which helped power us out of the recession of 1999-2003. Similarly, goods and services exports by the listed companies grew by an average of 24 per cent from 2008 to 2013, which helped power us out of the recession of 2007-08.

Business cycle recoveries in India are about surges in export demand and in investment demand. We do not know how bad the de-monetisation recession will be. But the timing for this was particularly unfortunate, given that one of the two pathways for recovery faces difficulties.

In India, we got a business cycle downturn in 2012. With demonetisation and difficult global conditions brought into the picture, the difficulties have deepened. Now the story will turn on the extent to which private firms get back into investing. This requires three things: capacity has to be utilised, profit margins have to be good, and the firm has to have the corporate financial depth to embark on large projects.

Source: *A Bad Time for Crisis* by Ajay Shah, Ajay Shah's blog, 12 December 2016.
URL. *http://www.mayin.org/ajayshah/MEDIA/2016/bad_time.html.*
Business Standard, 12 December 2016.

12

ILA PATNAIK

Crossing the Chasm

THE Reserve Bank of India's (RBI's) Monetary Policy Committee wisely decided not to cut policy rates in its meeting on 7 December. Though the economy has witnessed a sharp negative shock with a drop in consumer demand, a rate cut can do little to counter the shock of demonetisation. A policy rate decision is usually expected to have an impact on inflation in one to two years. By then, it is hoped that the impact of this negative demand shock will be over. Moreover, measuring the impact of demonetisation on inflation and the GDP is difficult as the story is still playing out. A bad, but not unlikely, scenario is that demonetisation increases uncertainty in the policy environment, and its effects go beyond the immediate demand reduction due to cash shortages. Consequently, it could lead to a postponement of investment revival by a few years making it difficult to forecast the GDP. Consequently, monetary policy-making too has gone into wait and watch mode.

The decision to keep the rate unchanged is also good as an attempt to improve public perception of the RBI. Demonetisation and its handling, as well as the RBI's insistence that the process was carefully deliberated, adequately prepared for, and that there is ample cash with banks, has undermined the public's confidence in the RBI's capabilities and its commitment to the inflation target. Deputy Governor R. Gandhi's statement after the monetary policy meeting raises, rather than answers, questions about the RBI's competence. Most are unconvinced that the RBI board's recommendation to the government to demonetise was based on independent and technically sound analysis.

As a way out of the shortage of cash, government and the RBI have appealed to the public to adopt electronic payments. Indeed, it increasingly appears as if that, rather than black money held in cash, was the main objective of demonetisation. One point often made in the current debate is the difficulty in doing so as half the Indian population is unbanked. This is an important obstacle in the adoption of electronic payments. The pertinent question, however, is: Why does half of India's population not have bank accounts?

Most of India lacks bank accounts because we have tried to apply a command and control approach to banking policy. The lack of a competitive banking system meant that banks themselves were not inclined to open rural branches and ask customers to open bank accounts. Instead, beginning with the nationalisation of banks, it has been a government initiative for many decades. Banks have been given targets. Pushing public sector banks to open branches, and then pushing them to open accounts for the poor has not been a successful strategy. We did not create a competitive banking system. New commercial bank licences have been rare, barely two per decade. Foreign banks are not allowed to open more than 20 branches a year.

No doubt, in these difficult days without cash, there will be some movement to digital payments. Growth figures, given today's tiny base, will look large. But even some of this may be temporary. Permanent adoption of electronic payment systems will depend on the ease of payments and the charges to be paid for these services. Government has made digital payments free till December end to alleviate the cash situation. At some point beyond that, payment service providers will be allowed to charge for their services otherwise they will shut down the service, killing the whole cashless project. It has been reported that Visa, Mastercard and RuPay will altogether lose ₹1,000 crore in November-December. Regardless of the accuracy of the amount reported, this is not a sustainable model.

Electronic payments have to be easy to adopt. There are plenty of models around the world to learn from. In some countries today, person to person payments are generally made digitally. Having effectively blocked such payments so far by onerous KYC (know your customer) norms and other restrictions, even the young who had the literacy, the means and the attitude to adopt e-payments, have not done so to the extent desired.

Unless the RBI ensures that all electronic payment systems and e-wallets are inter-operable, we could be creating a monopoly. Today the payments regulator, the RBI, prevents a Paytm customer from paying a MobiKwik customer. This is unlike the Telecom Regulatory Authority of India (TRAI) that pushes telecom companies to accept calls that originate from other telecom providers. A telecom company cannot refuse to accept incoming calls and force the customer receiving the call to subscribe to its service. However, a payments provider requires the customer receiving payments to download its app and become a subscriber.

In markets with such network externalities, one of the service providers is likely to emerge as a monopoly, unless the regulator steps in. This is undesirable for a number of reasons. It could leave customers vulnerable to higher charges later, which may again reduce the adoption of digital payments. Second, it would reduce the incentive of the monopolist to constantly innovate as he will not be facing competition. Third, it will create systemic risk as it will make the system vulnerable to the health and electronic infrastructure of one provider. If the provider fails, the whole system can crash and again the economy can come to a standstill.

If the government wishes to push faster for a cashless economy, policy and regulation need to focus on competition and innovation. The RBI has been promoting bank-centric payment systems in an economy where banks don't even compete to get customer accounts. It is no surprise that neither banking nor payments have spread to the entire population.

When you wish to influence the behaviour of millions of people, consumers, businesses there has to be a change in the policy framework from targets to one that works through incentives. In this case it has to be about incentives of banks, of payment service providers, of the payments regulator etc. Pushing the economy into cashlessness cannot be forced by putting ₹2,000 notes in the hands of the public so that people use electronic payments from lack of choice, where card companies provide the service at a loss and where some wallets could emerge as monopolies, from sheer neglect or not putting a competitive policy framework in place. If we are moving towards the goal of cashlessness, a focus on technology and neglect of an appropriate competitive regulatory framework will be short-sighted. The policy framework must be based on competition, interconnection and consumer protection. Policy work and committee processes have been working on cashlessness for many years. This work needs to go into the government's next steps.

Source: http://ilapatnaikblog.blogspot.in/2016/12/crossing-chasm.html; Indian Express, 09 December 2016.

13

T.C.A. SRINIVASA-RAGHAVAN

Three Shades of Black

THE intense disruption caused by the demonetisation of ₹500 and ₹1,000 notes has caused a massive debate on black money over the last two weeks. But much of it has been like that story about the blind men of "Hindoostan" who went around the elephant blindfolded and could not agree on what the creature was.

What everyone has overlooked is that in the nicer democracies there are only two types of black money. One is the hidden income of honest people. Another is the income—necessarily hidden—of criminals.

But India has a third type, and it is a "type"—or "class"—because of the large numbers involved of both persons and amounts. This is the income earned by the agents of the sovereign who earn via simple extortion to do what they are paid to do. Indeed, India is possibly the only country in the world where the employees of the sovereign extort each other as well. No one is spared.

When honest people hide a portion of their incomes, no one else suffers. Even with criminals only the victims suffer. But with India's third category, the servants of the sovereign, everyone suffers. They are exactly like a cancer. They spare no one, not even the dead at the cremation ground where they demand a bribe for dry wood.

It is perhaps because of this that people have been generally supportive of the demonetisation.

Three Shades

Much of the criticism of the decision to demonetise is because people tend to think of all three types at the same time and interchangeably. While the emotion is understandable, it is not very helpful in solving the problem of flow of black money.

Therefore, having attacked the stock of black money, and before he begins his onslaught on the flow of black money, Narendra Modi has to recognise the need for a different approach for each type. It will not be easy because he will have to use very considerable force.

This will have the politicians up on their hind legs, braying once again that democracy is in danger. Nothing could be further from the truth. Have no doubts: They are the main beneficiaries of black money.

As the law stands at present, it sanctions the use of considerable force only against the honest income earner who hides some part of his income because the various levies on income are so high.

Amazingly, where criminals are concerned, the government is less coercive. Many of them enjoy "protection", some of them even being MPs and others amoral businessmen who run away when they are held to account.

To tackle black money via tax evasion by the otherwise honest, Mr Modi must, absolutely must, reduce the extent to which the government picks their pockets. Income tax, GST, stamp duties, municipal taxes and, of course, the resulting corruption—all must come down.

Since GST is going to be around 18 per cent, income tax rates must be brought down to 15 and 25 per cent. The improvement in compliance will be enormous, as it was when P Chidambaram cut income taxes in 1997.

In India the government is very lenient with its own kind, namely, the various agents of the sovereign in Parliament, executive and judiciary. You can see this from the fact that the government's permission—rarely given—is required to prosecute a public servant. There are many other protections afforded to them as well, such as the process for impeachment.

That is why, if he wants to succeed fully, Mr Modi must go after this lot first, instead of allowing them to harass the generally honest income earners because the sheer inequity of it is mind-boggling: Utterly dishonest lawbreakers are entrusted with enforcing the law!

In his stump speeches, Mr Modi often reminds us of corruption in the government. But so far he has done precious little in tackling it. In fact, he seems scared of attacking those whose salaries come from the exchequer.

To put it baldly, it is the government that enables extortion which generated vast sums of black money. It is this Mr Modi has to tackle. Otherwise, demonetisation would have been a very expensive bet which he will lose.

Besides, there will be an added bonus: The silencing of Mr Chidambaram who, if he cares to recall, made extortion by tax officials easier by offering them a percentage of the tax they were instrumental in collecting.

This opened the doors for inflated notices and subsequent "adjustment".

Business Standard, 21 November 2016.

14

S.L. RAO

Black to White

Will it Stop Corruption?

THE Prime Minister in his election speeches and since 8 November is implying the black money has been the cause of nationwide corruption. In fact black money has been the outcome of corruption.

Black money has not paid taxes and does not feature in the national and tax accounts. While it is held as cash, it is also in *benami* bank accounts, converted into undeclared gold and jewellery, in real estate, and is also moved abroad and held there in bank accounts or as investments. Eliminating it requires rigorous investigation and honest prosecution. Both have been infrequent.

It arises out of bribery and corruption, tax evasion, smuggling and other criminal activities, but probably originated in a big way in the years of licence, controls and extortionate direct taxes on fairly low levels of income, introduced in the regime of Mrs Indira Gandhi. As government permissions and controls became more pervasive, the procedures and rules to enforce them became more complicated. Their interpretation and exercise by bureaucrats gave increasing opportunities for their application to be eased for a fee.

What do we have to do to minimise corruption in India? Our administrative systems must be revamped. Responsibility for actions and decisions must be attributed to individuals and not groups. Penalties for those caught must be made really severe. Positions must be for fixed terms and any shifts in between must be approved by an independent commission like the UPSC.

"Ease of doing business" must become a reality. An imperative is the essentiality of single window clearances. This must be in truth and not merely as words. A single officer must take responsibility for getting all clearances and anyone who does not have ample justification must face consequences for blocking speedy clearance. Making clearances and their progress transparent will help. The amount of regular reporting to government departments, inspections by different agencies, and other such government interferences must be reduced.

Allocations, leases, sales, of government owned resources (coal mines, telecom spectrum, etc.) must not be in secret but open. Major government contracts (for example, infrastructure purchases, etc.) must be transparent and preferably by auction. Quality of work must be independently assessed and publicly reported on a time schedule.

Government and its agencies are not merely sellers of valuable assets but buyers domestically and overseas. This has led to large scale corruption. One urgent step now under way is to try and manufacture such large items wholly or partly in India where they can be closely monitored. Another step would be to have each such transaction scrutinised quickly by the Comptroller and Auditor General (CAG) before placing an order.

There is also the large problem caused by money earned from corruption, paid abroad and overseas. As far as the first are concerned, government must exercise its agreements with other countries that such deposits in the names of Indians will be disclosed. A web of informers might be created in the principal countries where such moneys are deposited.

Moneys paid in India are many times sent abroad through hawala. There should be a separate agency to track down and close such hawala agents.

Money laundering is also done by sending these illegal earnings through hawala to countries like Mauritius from where they come back legally to India. These routes have been under this government's scrutiny. The government is working towards closing there routes in three years.

Much private purchasing and contracting are subject to over and under invoicing. Like the Enforcement Directorate, there must be an agency that watches such transactions to catch wrongdoers.

Multiple ministries for a common subject must go. Some examples are: Education—Primary, Secondary, Higher, Professional, Research, could all be together with a department for faculty training and development; Transport—to ensure coordinated development, road, rail, water, coastal shipping, must be in one Ministry; Similarly energy must include coal, power, atomic energy, renewable energy, petroleum and chemicals; in this way the number of Ministries can be reduced to ensure that there is full coordination.

This brief review must make it abundantly clear that black money and unaccounted money are only outputs of corruption. They can never be eliminated, only considerably reduced. For that to happen, many systemic reforms as indicated above, must take place.

Finally there is also lower level small time corruption—by police, postmen electricity meter readers, telephone mechanics, water supply operators, property valuers for taxes, school admissions, and many other things for which ordinary citizens have to deal with various government departments/agencies. Controlling black money is one step but needs many more big actions if corruption is to reduce.

Modi Government believes that the recent devaluing to zero of ₹500 and ₹1000 notes would soon eliminate black money and dent corruption. This is not merely optimistic but is also ignorant. It is thoughtless. There are many major actions to be thought through and implemented before we can get there. Demonetisation is a small step, poorly thought through and implemented.

15

RAJIV KUMAR

For Demonetisation to Work, Modi must Root Out Political and Bureaucratic Corruption

EVEN former prime minister Manmohan Singh, speaking in Rajya Sabha during the debate on demonetisation, admitted that its objectives were worthy of universal support. Moreover, people queuing up in front of banks for hours and 90 per cent of those responding to Prime Minister Modi's online survey have unequivocally supported the measure. This should have put to rest any doubts about the mass appeal of this measure. This near universal positive perception could, however, be based on a misperception of possible macroeconomic outcomes from demonetisation. Being undoubtedly the largest such exercise in the world, it has even drawn in international experts like Kenneth Rogoff and Larry Summers into the fray.

This is, therefore, an appropriate time to take stock of the on-going demonetisation.

The worst outcome of demonetisation, which has sucked out 86 per cent the total currency in circulation, could be that the cash crunch will kill those units operating in the informal sector, which work predominantly or exclusively with cash. The liquidity shortage could fatally affect both their input supplies and/or revenue flows. Added to the mayhem in the informal sector, farmers could be in severe distress if they can't sell their *kharif* harvest because of the cash shortage and as a consequence, be short of necessary agro-inputs for sowing *rabi* crops. The real estate sector will suffer from a precipitous fall in speculative and investment demand due to the attack on black money. And to top it all, consumption demand could collapse dramatically as consumption demand, especially ostentatious and luxury demand, takes a big hit as a result of demonetisation. All these negative impacts could effectively bring all economic activity to a grinding halt for the next six months or longer. This nightmare scenario is reflected in the forecast by Ambit Capital that India's GDP (gross domestic product) growth will halve to 3.5 per cent in 2016-17 with the third and fourth quarters (September to March) recording only 0.5 per cent growth. The slowdown will persist for the next two years, resulting undoubtedly in a resounding electoral defeat for Modi in 2019 general elections. According to these die-hard pessimists, Modi has dug his own political grave by implementing this measure. Has Modi been totally unaware of these grave downside risks when taking this step?

But Modi could have a different perspective. All informal sector enterprises essentially have some access to formal credit sources and only partially depend upon cash revenues for their survival. With more than 600 million account holders in the country, it is difficult to conceive of MSMEs (micro, small and medium enterprises) depending exclusively on cash for their sustenance. For example MSME units, which provide nearly 45 per cent of India's exports, necessarily operate with credit and through the banking system. They will certainly not be harmed by demonetisation. Moreover, with the impending introduction of GST (Goods and Service Tax) in the near future, a majority of MSME units are shifting to the formal economy to be able to take advantage of tax credits. These informal sector units could also realistically hope to secure their material inputs on credit terms, especially in such difficult times.

Payday Incoming

The crucial issue will be whether or not these informal sector enterprises are able to pay salaries to their employees in cash. An inability to do so, could result in acute and widespread deprivation and a backlash that could reverse the extant support for the move. The government must now urgently identify MSME clusters and export oriented units in labour-intensive sectors such as gems and jewellery, leather goods, garments, brassware and other handicrafts and ensure that their cash requirements for salary payments are fully met. This will prevent the ugly outcome of large numbers of workers in specific locations faced with extreme penury despite having toiled for a month and unable to access their legitimate salaries. If this impending salary crunch could be handled, a large majority of MSME enterprise could overcome the transient disruption and not suffer a mortal blow on their activity as the Cassandras forecast.

Farmers are not so badly affected. Nearly 80 per cent of rural households do not operate with 500 and 1,000 currency notes for their day to day activities. A hundred rupees still goes a fair way in the rural economy. Further, almost the entire *kharif* harvest of paddy can be sold to at government procurement counters at officially announced MSPs (minimum support prices). Sugarcane harvest is sold to sugar mills and their revenues traditionally credited to the farmers' bank accounts. From all reports so far, *rabi* sowing is on track because most if not all agro-inputs including tractors and harrows services are provided on 30-60 day credit. Temporary inconvenience yes, but there is no real economic distress in the agriculture sector. The only segment to suffer are the middlemen or the *arthiyas*, who have traditionally not only operated with cash but also generated large quantum of black incomes from their callous and age-old exploitation of Indian farmers.

Recent reports from the real estate sector are that demand has suddenly shot up with property developers obliging black money holders with back-dated purchases paid in 'old currency'. This is surely an illegal blip in housing demand and the real estate sector will suffer from the loss of black incomes and cash shortages, However, it has also been evident during the last three years that the withdrawal of speculative demand has been confined to major metros and has not affected housing and real estate demand in tier one and tier two cities and towns. The demand for housing in these smaller urban centres has been buoyant and is expected to remain so in the coming period. The government can feasibly ratchet up its expenditure to boost real estate and housing demand and take advantage of its extensive linkages and multiplier impact to boost aggregate demand.

Incoming Losses

This extreme downside risk to economic growth arising from demand weakness and supply side disruption will unfold in the third and fourth quarters of the current financial year, 2016-17. According to Manmohan Singh, we could see a decline of 2 per cent in GDP growth, which would then come in at 5.5 per cent instead of 7.5 per cent as generally estimate prior to demonetisation. Singh's estimate of a decline in GDP growth would imply a one-off loss of nearly ₹27 lakh crore to the economy. This will surely be accompanied by job losses across sectors but concentrated perhaps in real estate, wholesale and retail trade, production units in the informal sector and intermediate services like transport and logistics. These costs would be justified only if demonetisation is seen as the first step in eliminating the malignancy of black economy.

The government can try to minimise these losses by following some steps. It can stagger the period of using the old currency for a longer period and also for a larger number of users than permitted at present. The period for depositing the currency notes could be extended beyond 31 December, to provide more time for residents in far-flung villages to deposit their holdings of old currency and relieve the current pressure on commercial bank branches. The government should actively consider steps to augment the supply of currency by importing it if necessary. They must rope in various departments and agencies as distribution centres for the new currency, especially for its own employees and affiliated agencies. This opportunity could be used to accelerate the adoption of digital payment methods that are already in use. This could see India leapfrog other economies in the area of 'fintech.' Finally, it is surprising that there have been no arrests so far for people trying to spuriously exchange money or depositing huge amounts in Jan Dhan deposits. This needs to be reversed.

An upside scenario also deserves attention. Rather than result in a dead loss to the economy of 2 per cent of GDP, demonetisation could actually yield a fairly strong fillip to economic activity. With commercial banks now flush with nearly ₹6 lakh crore of additional deposits, short-term lending rates have already trended downwards rather sharply. It is true that a very large part of these deposits will be needed in due course to meet liquidity requirements, but some additionality in deposits is a near certainty. Lower interest rates on saving deposits will be followed by a reduction in lending rates on working capital loans immediately and term loans subsequently. A reduction in capital costs will help make Indian firms globally competitive.

More importantly, five structural changes that will boost GDP growth rates may well take place as a direct consequence of demonetisation. One, the currency preference of the general public will surely weaken after this event, thereby bringing down the currency to GDP ratio. This is high in India at 12 per cent as compared to an average of 4-5 per cent in other emerging economies and 7 per cent in the US, notorious for its cash preference. This will reduce costs of currency printing and also reduce the space for black money. A related gain will be to eliminate counterfeit currency that has been used for financing terrorist and extremist organisations. Costs of producing the counterfeit currency will increase substantially.

Second, the move will provide a strong fillip to digital payment methods. Given our (Indians) somewhat surprising affinity to and ability for adopting innovative practices, a shift is already underway and will most likely spread in double time. This will also hasten the adoption of Unified Payment Interface (UPI), promoted by the National Payment Corporation. UPI enables subscribers, at no extra cost, to digitally transfer (pay and receive) money from their deposits either to vendors and other individuals. With 26 commercial banks already on board and the clear prospect of behemoths like State Bank of India (SBI) joining the platform, UPI could well help India surge ahead in the adoption of digital money. With Prime Minister Modi himself promoting its adoption in public rallies, this could see a very rapid adoption of digital cash transfers in keeping with greater penetration of smartphones and Internet. The direct implication will be a further constriction of the space for black money and generation of parallel economy.

Third, it is estimated that up to ₹4.5-5.0 lakh crore ($74 billion) may not find its way back to the banking system. These estimate would change in light of the latest announcement by the government that black money hoarders would be permitted to hold on to 40 per cent of their holdings in bank deposits with a lock-in period of three years and carrying zero interest. However, to the extent that some black currency will be 'killed', it will represent a windfall gain for the government as the liability represented by the quantum of 'non-returned currency' will be permanently extinguished. This could be used in several different ways to increase the fiscal space for the government for ramping up public expenditure and by the Reserve Bank of India (RBI) to sharply cut interest rates.

Fourth, demonetisation will also lower the price of urban land and real estate. In conjunction with lower costs of capital, this will ceteris paribus, encourage investment and switch the Indian growth story from its dependence on domestic consumption to being investment driven. This would be far more sustainable and also more employment generating.

Finally, faced with the loss of domestic purchasing power, Indian entrepreneurs would be forced to look more actively and aggressively for export markets. India could enter a period in which the past trend of net exports being perpetually negative would be reversed and India's presently measly share of 1.6 per cent in global merchandise trade could rise. This would also contribute to the all-important task of generating employment in a country that will see the addition of at least one million new workers every month for the next 15 years.

Like Dominoes

All these five positive outcomes, however, depend crucially on whether this first step of demonetisation is followed by others that are aimed at rooting out political and bureaucratic corruption. These are the fountain-heads of black incomes and also quite often the principal cause of honest businessmen resorting to corrupt practices. The prime minister has, on several occasions assured on this count and one hopes that these assurances will be honoured. Some steps have already been implemented. These include, making the industrial licensing system more transparent and less discretionary;

implementing the GST; linking bank accounts to Aadhaar; making Aadhaar and pan card numbers compulsory for large value purchases; the passing of Benami Property Act and its early implementation etc. All these will surely make the generation of black and illegal incomes more difficult in future and reduce the space and scope for the parallel economy.

One warning. The government has to ensure and assure the people that they will not be hounded and terrorised by the income tax bureaucracy that may see itself as having been doubly empowered. Some ominous signs of this 'taxman' overreach and harassment are already visible. Apprehending culprits and money launderers will have to be done most cautiously and with due care for not harassing the professionals, common businessman, traders and entrepreneurs. Prime Minister Modi must make it clear to the income tax officials that it is only a simple, rational and non-threatening tax process that engenders much-needed taxpayers' confidence in the system. Taxpayer cooperation will not be achieved through persistent threats of harassment and exploitation. I am afraid the income tax department has not so far covered itself with glory on this count. On the contrary, stories of their patently unacceptable boorish and downright inhuman behaviour during income tax 'raids and searches' are legion. This raid and seizure culture and practices must change if we are to become a civilised and honest society, which successfully eliminated the pernicious illegal economy.

Simultaneously, measures will have to be initiated to roll back political corruption that generates black money. The principle cause for this is undoubtedly the need for slush funds for election campaign finance. Many solid suggestions to curb and root out the need for black money for financing election campaigns have been made including most recently by B.J. Panda, a Biju Janta Dal (BJD) MP. The prime minister has all the wherewithal to implement this critical change as well. He has near total control over his own party; has a large majority in the Lok Sabha and the Bharatiya Janata Party (BJP) could have a sizeable presence in the Rajya Sabha after the next round of provincial elections. Modi has also developed a strong direct connect with the people to whom he could appeal to overcome any political resistance to his proposals to make election campaign financing more transparent and accountable.

If these two critical steps of reigning in the income tax bureaucracy and cleansing the election campaign process are implemented, Modi will certainly usher in the golden period in India's economic development. We will become attractive for both domestic and foreign investors with a relatively corruption free environment that offers predictability and accountability. It will provide the positive encouragement for honest workers and professionals who will not see themselves as constantly lagging behind their corrupt peers. India could regain its ethical and moral elan. A golden period for the Indian economy could then ensue and see the economy achieve double-digit growth for a sustained period.

Without these follow-up measures, I am afraid, a great opportunity would have been wasted. It would then be difficult for Modi to counter the charge, currently being hurled at him by those who oppose this move, that demonetisation with all its attendant pains and disruptions was not undertaken for serving national interest but instead to serve some narrower political and personal agenda. I am convinced that Modi, who knows the score all too well, will not let down the common Indian who has supported him despite the pain and inconvenience he has suffered in the wake of 'currency surgical strike' on 8/11.

Source: https://thewire.in/83286/for-demonetisation-to-work-modi-must-root-out-political-and-bureacratic-corruption/.

16

NITIN DESAI

Towards Swaccha Chunav

THE massive demonetisation exercise undertaken by the government has caused widespread disruption of cash transactions. Much of the focus right now is, quite rightly, on mitigating the short term pain being suffered by the innocent. It is also probable that only a small proportion of black wealth will be destroyed as most of it is held in other forms like *benami* property and undeclared bullion or foreign assets.

The big impact could be on future flows. The disruption of cash transactions will hit all illegal activities and even some legal ones that seek to stay out of the tax net or the public eye. This disruption must be used to secure the longer term policy and institutional changes that constrain sufficiently the reemergence of these malpractices.

One such area is the financing of elections by candidates and political parties. In the past, the United Progressive Alliance (UPA) took over two columns on this subject.[1] This column is more or less a reiteration of these decade old plaints and proposals. But now, with the parties singed by the fire of demonetisation, there may be a greater willingness to consider a major reform in this area.

Proposals for public funding of candidates and parties have been on the table for quite some time. But citizens and taxpayers will not accept this to finance family fiefdoms or parties that take public funds but continue to draw in undeclared private money as well.

The source of power in the many family controlled political parties that are thriving is control over money. In these satrapies the sources and uses of party funds is opaque not just to the public

1. "The Politics of Corruption" *Business Standard*, 16 March 2005 and "Paying for Politics" *Business Standard*, 20 April 2005.

and the regulators but also to party members. Much of this comes as secret contributions from profit seekers seeking unjustifiable preferences in purchase and construction contracts, or appointments and postings, or policy changes designed to aid them vis-à-vis some competitor. It may even take the form of outright extortion. Worse still, it may involve turning a blind eye to criminal activities.

The rot in political funding goes beyond the family controlled parties. Take election funding. The law as recently amended permits candidates an expenditure of around ₹4 per voter in Lok Sabha elections. This is laughable. Even the administrative cost of running the 2014 election amounted to over ₹40 per voter according to Election Commission estimates. The major political parties (BJP, INC, BSP, NCP, CPM, CPI) reported expenditure of ₹1,897 crore in this election year. Informed estimates put the spending in the 2014 Lok Sabha election at around ₹30,000 crore. As for sources of funds ₹1,130 crore came from unknown sources. Frankly the law on election spending and the reporting procedure is a farce.

Public funding of candidates or parties requires a more credible law on spending and a much tougher monitoring process than at present. It has to go hand in hand with a radical reforms in the functioning of political parties. Public funds should only go to parties that meet certain mandatory standards of inner party democracy and transparency in their income and expenditure.

Public funding of parties and candidates is quite common in democracies. According to an international database 130 countries provide direct public funding to political parties. In a large number of countries public funds are provided regardless of whether an election is imminent or not; but in some countries public funding kicks in only for elections. Generally the funding is made available to the political party rather than the candidate, though the distinction is tenuous in a presidential system like the USA. In Canada, which has a parliamentary system, there are two separate categories of election subsidy, one for individual parliamentary candidates, the other for the national party organisations.

In India the norms for public funding will have to be designed to be consistent with the right of any eligible citizen to stand for election and at the same time not support fraudulent efforts to stand for election or constitute a party simply to secure the public largesse.

Parties must be required to establish their credibility by mobilising resources directly from their members and supporters, at least for routine organisational purposes. The focus of public funding should be on the high costs incurred by parties to fight elections.

To repeat the proposal from eleven years ago, a two-part election funding system could be considered. The first part would give a certain amount of money to recognised political parties in proportion to the votes secured by them in the seats where they won or saved their deposits. The seats which they contest, but where they lose their deposits, have to be ignored. This is to prevent parties from putting up candidates in hopeless seats simply to increase their vote tally. The second part would give funds to all candidates who save their deposits so as to make it easier to challenge the incumbents without having to finance the less credible and possibly frivolous candidates.

Public funding need not rule out transparent private funding, say by business lobbies or trade unions, where regulatory disclosures and a watchful media would allow voters to make their own judgements on what such funding implies.

How can such a change be brought about? If we leave it to Parliament than the differing interests of national and regional parties and of party hierarchies and individual parliamentarians will lead to a stalemate. A committee of former Chief Election Commissioners could be asked to recommend the modalities of funding and the mandatory standards of democratic functioning and financial transparency which parties have to follow to be eligible for public funding.

Putting an end to political corruption will be a game changer for our democracy and law and order as it will break the politician criminal nexus. The economy will gain as it will reduce egregious policy distortions, high-level bureaucratic corruption and black money generation in transactions that depend on discretionary official patronage.

So let the next Modi slogan be 'Swaccha Chunav' and the target be a clean election in 2019.

Business Standard, 24 November 2016.

17

M. GOVINDA RAO

Demonetisation

The Gains vis-à-vis the Pains

THE announcement by the prime minister on 8th November that currency notes with face-value of ₹500 and ₹1,000 will no longer be valid sent shock-waves. The discussion on the difficulties and questions relating to selective demonetisation refuses to die down any time soon. This should have been expected as in an economy where over 96 per cent of transactions are carried out in cash, rendering 86 per cent of the currency useless with such sleight of hand cannot but plunge the economy into a chaotic spin. The people have been patient and enduring, but the question on everyone's mind is: For how long? The prime minister, in his broadcast, had asked for forbearance for 50 days, but it remains to be seen whether normalcy can return by then.

Ostensibly, the measure was taken with the principal objective of curbing black economy, though other objectives like ending terror-financing and nullifying the counterfeit notes were also mentioned. While there cannot be any quarrel with the objectives, the two important questions are: (i) whether demonetising 86 per cent of currency in circulation makes a sound policy choice to achieve the objectives, and (ii) has the government taken into account the capacity of RBI to remonetise within a reasonable time period and of the banking system to implement such a policy.

As far as the first question is concerned, it must be said that selective demonetisation of the type undertaken is neither necessary nor is it sufficient to deal with the menace. First, the measure by itself will not have any impact on the incentives to generate black money and it does not deter earning illegal incomes and evade taxes.

The principal sources of black economy generation in activities like political funding and election expenses, real estate transactions, construction, tax evasion and bureaucratic corruption will continue. It is argued that there will be additional policy initiatives to deal with the generation of black economy. If so, those measures should have been initiated first as they are independent of demonetisation and would have impacted on the process of generating black money and would not have inflicted pain and misery on the poor and vulnerable.

Second, the measure will not have much impact on the stock of black economy as not all currency accumulation is illegal and the overwhelming proportion of the black economy is either stashed abroad or held in real estates and gold and foreign currency. The White Paper brought out by the ministry of finance in 2012 states that, the extent of cash revealed in various search and seizure operations between 2006 and 2012 was 3.8-7.3 per cent. The generous estimate is that only about 5-6 per cent of the black economy is held in cash and only a small proportion of this may not find its way into the banks. It is reported that already over ₹11 trillion of ₹14 trillion has been deposited in the banks and the volume of invalid currency not coming back into the system is yet to be seen. Admittedly, there are stories about round-tripping by measures like surrogate accounts, laundering through the North-East route, converting by using paid labour and advance payments. The capacity of income tax administration to unravel these remains to be seen and surely, quite a few of the cases will end up in already overburdened courts.

If the government is serious about tackling the menace of black money, it should begin with cleaning political funding. The high moral ground taken by the prime minister will be amply justified if the ruling party throws open its books of accounts to independent audit and subjects itself to the Right to Information Act. In 2013, the Central Information Commission ruled that political parties are public authorities and yet, all the six national parties (except the Left) closed their ranks to violate the ruling by rejecting the right to information. The donations to political parties have continued to be opaque and the limits on election expenses are violated with impunity. The Election Commission has laid down the ceiling on election expenses at ₹70 lakh for a Parliament seat and ₹28 lakh for a seat in Legislature for the candidates, but there is no restriction on the spending by political parties. *The Hindu* estimated that, as against a declaration of ₹7,000 crore by candidates in the 2014 general election, the estimated expenditure was ₹30,000 crore.

Besides the reform of political funding, the abolition of the capital gains tax and reduction of stamp duties by the states to 3 per cent will substantially reduce the black money generated in real estate transactions. Similarly, simplification of laws and procedures to reduce the discretion by bureaucracy will help a great deal in reducing bureaucratic corruption. The clearances required for construction abound. We keep reading about the huge corruption in defence purchases. We are well aware of the goings-on in the Medical Council of India and, despite the NITI Aayog revealing much that is wrong, the government is yet to act on it. The situation is not very different in the case of higher and technical education.

It is obvious that a shock-therapy of such a magnitude can be implemented with some measure of comfort by the banking system. Over 30 per cent of the people employed in India are casual and contract labourers who receive their wages, and pay for purchases, in cash; they have been put to severe hardship, often losing their wages while standing in the queues. This has also adversely impacted trade, tourism, small-scale manufacturing and construction activities. The shock-therapy has come at just about the time when *rabi* sowing is in progress and farmers are finding it difficult to purchase seeds and fertilisers. It is estimated that remonetising about ₹12 trillion as against the prevailing ₹14.18 trillion at the present capacity of the printing presses would take not less than 175 days.

The release of the second quarter GDP shows that the economy has virtually been stagnant and all sectors, except agricultural, have decelerated. In fact, the growth of GVA (gross value added), which is a better measure than GDP, despite the better performance of agricultural sector in the second quarter has slowed down from 7.3 per cent in the first quarter to 7.1 per cent in the second. With the GDP growth during the first two quarters at about 7.2 per cent, RBI's forecast of 7.6 per cent for the year can be realised only if the growth rate in the next two quarters averages 8.2 per cent. With trade, tourism, small-scale manufacturing and construction activity coming to a standstill and with agricultural sector starved of cash for purchasing seeds and fertilisers for *rabi* sowing, the country's GDP will decelerate significantly. At a time when gross fixed capital formation relative to GDP showing a decline from 32 per cent to 29 per cent and growth is primarily fuelled by private consumption, the selective demonetisation has hurt the growth prospects significantly in this quarter and the next.

18

YOGINDER K. ALAGH

Demonetisation

Then, Now and Next Year

DEMONETISATION of five hundred and one thousand rupee notes this week is a big event; obviously a game changer. At one stroke, tax evaders and other such people who were not keeping their wealth in gold, land or dollars were dealt a lethal blow. Some would distribute currency to their relatives or servants but for the larger operator, this had very limited scope. There has been discussion that this was done in 1978, around 40 years ago.

Prime Minister Morarji Desai decided, as Gujarati Prime Minister's do, to demonetise high value notes. In those days he took up a really high value one, namely the one thousand rupee note. I vividly remember, a conversation then which now has contemporary relevance. Dr I.G. Patel then Governor Reserve Bank of India, told Prime Minister Morarji Desai in chaste Gujarati, "Sahib, this (the demonetisation of the thousand rupee notes) will not work, black money is held in land, gold and dollars because they appreciate in value and not in currency." The late H.M. Patel then Finance Minister was present and was smiling away at this exchange. Morarji bhai would have none of this and went ahead. When we now talk about that demonetisation episode, of a thousand rupee notes in some sense as comparable to today we make a great mistake. It has to be remembered that the currency cut off point then was much higher. In those days, the price of gold was around ₹600 for 10 grams. It is now around ₹30,000 per 10 grams and since gold is a good measure of the value of the money in classical monetary theory, a thousand rupee note then would be worth roughly fifty thousand rupees now and so the coverage of demonetisation in the present exercise is much greater. In those days a middle class housewife would not have thousand rupee notes to tuck way from her savings from kitchen money. Look at it otherwise. A thousand rupee note then equals a twenty rupee note now. Today she does save five hundred or thousand rupee notes. As a friend's wife told me if he has a heart attack at night and I have to take him to a hospital they want a lakh of rupees in cash as a deposit before they admit him to the ICU. The remonetisation of the economy has to be deep now. Eighty per cent of our economy it is estimated works with cash. Financial intermediation is for the remaining 20 per cent. This ratio is higher than in most developing economies but much lower than the rich countries where cash accounts for 10 per cent of the cash economy. So the economic pain is much higher. To aim in the short run at the monetisation of economy according to the standards of a developed economy when the problem is to build up the infrastructure including that of financial intermediation to reach there, is not very practical. There is no point in blaming the hapless Governor of the central bank who is perhaps one of the best experts on financial intermediation and development, anywhere. The demand for currency is high and you can't deliver it instantaneously with non-existing infrastructure. Throwing currency notes from a helicopter is a standard tool of teaching monetary economics but not a very practical solution in the real world.

To the best of my knowledge, I was the first one to make a distinction between the stock of black money which was destroyed last week and the flow, and my argument was that we need to plug the flow and this argument has been highlighted by most experts since. Otherwise black money would start being generated with the new notes once they are available in plenty which may be so towards the end of the month. If everything else remains the same we will have plenty of new currency and the same actors and markets will start functioning again. The only outcome would be the pain the housewife went through. But hopefully this will not be so. The Prime Minister has reportedly said that unaccounted money used in real estate and land deals will be targeted. We need similar plans for gold and foreign exchange in hawala. The crispiness and sexy colours of the new notes will not deter the operators. The sooner the Government shares the details of their pre-emptive plans for these possible illegal activities the more comforted we will all be that our pain is not in vain. Also, it will be comforting to know that great political leaders changing sides like in the States where this has happened in the recent past are really doing so because of their political conviction and not for a mess of pottage as the Bard said. Of course if we selectively hit black marketers, a general demonetisation may not have been needed, but that is another story.

By now it is clear the economy has gone through a major haircut. To me, the most important issue and the first action point is restoration of faith in currency. As the process of financial intermediation expands in an economy through the integration of money markets with the growth process, the role of currency declines. The definition of money itself includes bank deposits and currency substitutes. But the entire edifice is based on the expansion of currency as its foundation. We have literally proved that currency without faith in it, is just a piece of paper. Grandma saved out of her kitchen money and set aside notes for the rainy day. We are at our level of income high savers. For example Pakistanis save half as much as we do out of their income. Now grandma will worry that any day the finance minister will declare her notes as not being kosher and she will first have to tell everybody what she had done and then the hassle of standing in a queue.

The Government and the central bank have to sustain this confidence in the currency and the Governor of the central bank is to be congratulated on stating that everybody's financial wealth is safe in banks. Caution would be commendable in political statements on currency. The need is to support confidence rather than instil fears.

Is it possible for the economy to recover in the fourth quarter? This question is not up in the stars for astrologers to decipher, but in the hands of the men and women who make policy and run monetary and banking systems. The sooner we begin discussion on the recovery of the economy in terms of business like projects and policies as compared to the excruciating haircut, the better of we will be. Mere words will not do and this has to be based on restoring confidence and establishing the contours of the revival in language that the people understand.The vast majority of workers, traders, service agents and consumers are hardworking consciencous people who have been made to suffer on account of the mismanagement of the law makers. The package in the next budget must be to revive growth and has to be the centre of attention. It will have to consist essentially the reviving of public investment in infrastructure on a massive scale. There is great slack in the system. Skilled labour has gone to the *gaon* and *desh* and is only a mobile call away. Factories, shops and all are full of unused capabilities, waiting for signals. The formulation that some Government economists have been advocating that a reform package which consists of easing the import of gold, making real estate investments cheaper and measures of this kind are quixotic. The economy will not respond to such measures. It is also true that the revival of the economy will be a painful process. The Monetary Policy Committee of the central bank has approved the caution in not reducing interest rates as widely expected in the financial press. The earlier speculation that monetary reserves could be credited on account of the destruction of currency is by now seen as extremely unlikely. In other words the economy will have to face the classical problems of expanding demand, utilising surplus capacity and keeping an eye on rising costs in some sectors. This will be painful. The sooner we have a road map, the better off we will all be.

19

PRAVEEN CHAKRAVARTY

Cashless/Digital

How Modi Changed (and Changed) Demonetisation Narrative

PRIME Minister Narendra Modi addressed the nation on 8 November 2016 to announce the withdrawal of ₹500 and ₹1,000 notes.

The speech (in English) lasted 25 minutes. The Prime Minister uttered the phrase "black money" 18 times in this speech. He mentioned "fake currency" or "counterfeit" 5 times in the same speech.

It was unambiguously clear from the Prime Minister's speech that the primary motivation for the sudden withdrawal of nearly 86 per cent of the country's currency was the evil of black money.

The next day, the papers termed it a "war on black money". PayTM, a mobile payment app, hailed the decision with a full-page ad and the Prime Minister left for Japan.

By the time the Prime Minister returned from Japan, the move had been christened "demonetisation" in English, "notebandi" in Hindi and there was a war-time like rationing of currency in the country.

The Prime Minister made six speeches across the country on the demonetisation policy between 13 November and 27 November, including his radio address to the nation, *Mann Ki Baat*, according to data available on the Prime Minister's personal website. The text of all the speeches are available on the website.

Author thanks Puja Das of IndiaSpend for help with Hindi translation.

A data analysis of the speeches (after translation) reveals a shifting of the narrative of the demonetisation action and its objectives.

In his speech on 8 November 2016, when he announced the demonetisation policy, the Prime Minister used the phrase "black money" four times more than "fake/counterfeit currency".

By 27 November, he used the phrase "digital/cashless" thrice as much as "black money" with no mention of "fake currency". Recall, there was zero mention of "digital/cashless" in the initial 8 November speech.

Figure 19.1 shows the ratio of the three narratives—"black money", "fake currency" and "cashless/digital pay"—in each of the Prime Minister's speeches over three weeks and seven speeches.

Figure 19.1

Progression of Keywords in the Prime Minister's Speeches

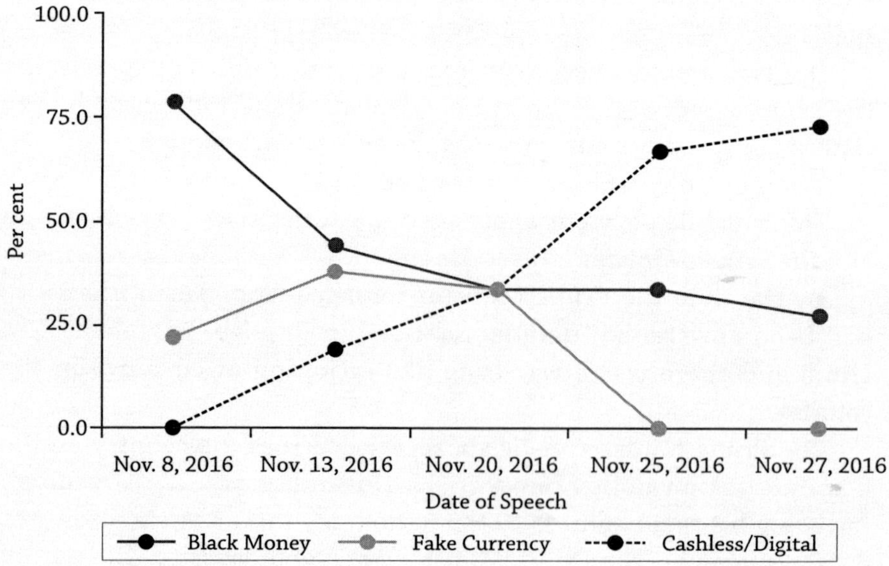

In other words, in the same speech, how many times did the Prime Minister use each of these phrases to describe the reasons for demonetisation which can be used as a proxy to understand what the

Prime Minister believes was the primary objective for this mammoth exercise.

The dotted line representing the "cashless/digital" phrase in the Prime Minister's speeches went from 0 in the 8 November speech to a 73 per cent ratio in the 27 November speech.

The grey line representing the phrase "fake currency" went from 22 per cent to 0 in the same period suggesting the Prime Minister no longer believes that terror financing was the primary or secondary driver of this demonetisation exercise.

The black line representing the phrase "black money" went from a high of a 80 per cent ratio on 8 November to only 27 per cent on 27 November. Apparently, it is no longer a "war on black money" but instead a "war on all currency" to go cashless.

So, between 8 November and 27 November, the objective for the demonetisation exercise has swung from black money elimination to going cashless, as evident in the Prime Minister's speeches.

To be sure, urging citizens to use less cash and resort to digital transactions is a laudable objective and must certainly be encouraged. But when a decision was taken to remove a whopping 86 per cent of the country's currency overnight with all its attendant costs, one would have hoped there was one strong rationale for it, even if it meant achieving multiple objectives.

Either the Prime Minister has realised that the original primary objective of eliminating black money may not be met or there was not adequate thought behind the decision. Either way, it is worrisome.

Business Standard, 05 December 2016.

20

RADHIKA PANDEY and BHARGAVI ZAVERI

Legal Questions about Demonetisation

What Happens to the Assets that Back Extinguished Rupee Notes

THERE are three important questions of law[1] associated with demonetisation. This article seeks to shed some light on the third question. The demonetisation of ₹500 and ₹1000 has led to speculation[2] about the amount of currency that will not be deposited or exchanged at all, because of fear of scrutiny by tax authorities. Some[3,4,5] suggest that from and out of the notes in circulation, close to 20 per cent may not be exchanged or deposited at all with RBI. (Others[6] believe this will not happen). The numerical values involved are very large; 20 per cent works out to INR 3 trillion disappearing from circulation.

The law governing the withdrawal of legal tender in India allows the Central Government to declare that currency notes of a certain denomination will not be legal tender, except at the specified offices of RBI until such date as may be specified by the Central Government in

1. *https://ajayshahblog.blogspot.in/2016/11/questions-of-law-in-demonetisation.html*
2. *http://www.business-standard.com/article/opinion/manish-sabharwal-why-demonetisation-will-work-116111401650_1.html*
3. *http://indianexpress.com/article/business/banking-and-finance/rs-1000-rs-500-note-exchange-20-per-cent-no-show-may-lead-to-rs-3-lakh-crore-black-money-destruction-4367271/*
4. *http://www.livemint.com/Politics/GBzL9d8x9Ms3it1epq9MzM/Subbarao-warns-RBI-against-taking-unclaimed-notes-as-profit.html*
5. *http://www.business-standard.com/article/opinion/t-n-ninan-socialist-bonanza-116111100957_1.html*
6. *http://www.bloombergquint.com/business/2016/11/16/shock-to-money-supply-can-have-economy-wide-implications-ajay-shah*

a gazetted notification. In his speech,[7] the Prime Minister specified 31 March 2017 as the date up to which RBI will accept the demonetised currency. However, in our knowledge, this date has not appeared in a gazetted notification.[8] Let's assume that RBI will cease to be liable to accept the un-returned demonetised notes after a certain date, which for the time being, appears to be 31 March 2017.

The central bank of any country must, for every note that it issues, back itself with corresponding assets. The liability incurred on notes issued and the assets backing such liability, are reflected in the balance sheet of the central bank. Typically, these assets are government securities, bullion and foreign securities. Now, in a one-time event like demonetisation, the liabilities of the central bank may significantly plummet, as the central bank will no longer require to honour the commitment to pay on the notes that are not returned to it. This would lead to a mismatch in the balance sheet of the central bank.

In the past, we have seen such gains being made in other countries that have substituted currency. For instance, the Bank of Israel recorded again of about USD 62 million[9] for the notes that had passed the legal date for exchange and were no longer in use. There is considerable public discourse[10] on what will happen to the windfall made by RBI, if the above mentioned estimates were to translate into reality.

In this article, we argue that unlike several other countries with precise laws governing their central banks, there is legal uncertainty on what happens to the surplus reserves or income accruing to RBI, whether as a result of a one-time demonetisation event or due to its regular operations. There is a need to re-visit the legal framework governing surplus distribution by RBI.

---

7. *http://blogs.wsj.com/indiarealtime/2016/11/08/full-text-of-indian-prime-minister-narendra-modis-speech-on-replacing-largest-rupee-notes/*
8. *http://finmin.nic.in/172521.pdf*
9. *https://home.kpmg.com/xx/en/home/insights.html*
10. *http://www.business-standard.com/article/economy-policy/demonetisation-no-windfall-gain-deploying-anytime-soon-116111601868_1.html*

Lack of Clarity in Distribution Policy

Ordinarily, when a mismatch occurs on the balance sheet of a corporation due to a sudden change in the liabilities, the resulting surplus assets are either (a) distributed as dividend to the shareholders; or (b) credited to reserves. This takes place under the rubric of a `dividend distribution policy', which is generally voted upon by the board. The circumstances in which shareholders should or should not expect dividend, and the manner in which the retained earnings will be utilised, are generally codified in the dividend distribution policy. The policy is disclosed to the shareholders, so as to enhance predictability, and governs their relationship with the corporation.

Likewise, where a central bank has surplus reserves or profits in any given financial year (whether due to a one-time event like demonetisation or otherwise in the course of its regular operations), the shareholders of the central bank (in a majority of the cases, the government) must have clarity on the distribution policy. This must be clearly spelt out to the Central Government in the law governing its relationship with RBI or in an agreement between them that is available in public domain. This is critical to ensure both (a) the independence of RBI as it pre-empts any possiblity of political pressure for distribution of surplus profits or reserves; and (b) accountability of both the RBI and the Central Government with regard to the distribution of surplus profits to the Consolidated Fund of India.

Currently, this clarity is missing. As a result, the distribution of surplus assets by RBI to the Central Government has fluctuated year-on-year, except for the last three financial years, as shown in Figure 20.1.

Figure 20.1 shows that the proportion of profits transferred to the Central Government has fluctuated across the years. However, for the last three financial years, the distribution has remained constant at 99.9 per cent due to the recommendations of the Report of the Technical Committee to review the level and adequacy of internal reserves and surplus distribution policy[11] (hereafter, the Malegam

11. *https://www.rbi.org.in/scripts/AnnualReportPublications.aspx?Id=1130*

Committee Report, which is discussed in greater detail later in this article).

Figure 20.1

Transfer to Government of India, by RBI
(% to Profits)

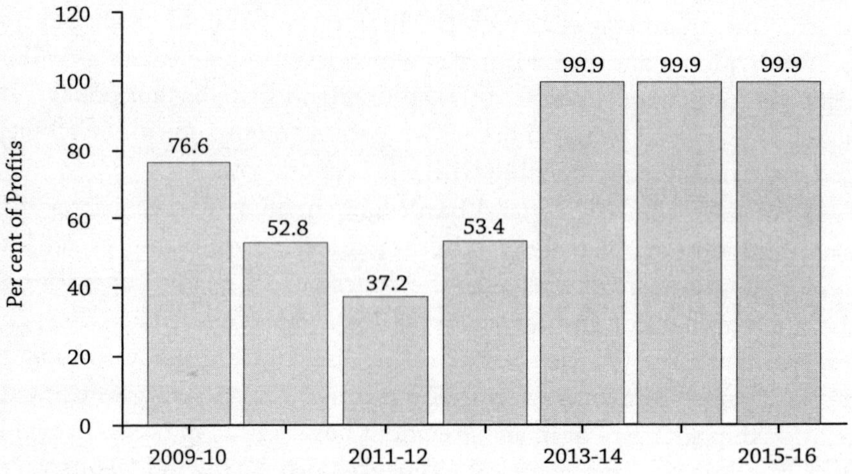

What does the Law Say?

In India, the relationship between the RBI and its sole shareholder, ie. the Central Government, is governed by the Reserve Bank of India Act, 1934 (RBI Act). As currently drafted, the provision governing allocation of surplus profits lacks details on the reserves that RBI must maintain and the proportion of surplus that RBI must distribute to the Central Government. The RBI Act contains one provision on allocation of surplus profits. Section 47 of the RBI Act says:

> After making provision for bad and doubtful debts, depreciation in assets, contributions to staff and superannuation funds and for all other matters for which provision is to be made by or under this Act or which are usually provided for by bankers, the balance of the profits shall be paid to the Central Government.

The provision implies two things (a) surplus is only the amount which is left after RBI has made adequate provision for all other matters for which provision is to be made (i) under the RBI Act or (ii) for matters which are usually provided for by bankers; and (b) the entire residual surplus shallbe paid to the Central Government. There is no clarity in the RBI Act on:

1. the proportion of profits which may be allocated to reserve funds or the purpose of the reserve funds;
2. the cap, if any, on reserves;
3. the proportion of profits which must be distributed to the Central Government;
4. the timing of distribution of profits;
5. the manner in which these decisions must be made.

The current legal framework is, therefore, inadequate as it offers no transparency with regard to these matters.

What do Central Banks Around the World do with their Profits and Surplus Assets?

Laws governing several central banks around the world have a numerical value, which offers clarity on the distribution policy. Several legal frameworks governing central banks across the world, precisely state the proportion of surplus assets that must be credited to the reserves, the proportion that must be distributed to the exchequer, the timing of distribution, etc. Some examples are listed below:

1. *Specifying the percentage of profit which must be distributed:* Some laws governing central banks mandate the specific percentage of net profits which must be distributed by the central bank. For instance, the Bank of England Act, 1946 requires the Bank of England (BOE) to pay to the Exchequer, on every 5th April and 5th October, a sum equal to 25 per cent of BOE's net profits for its previous financial year, or such other sum as the Treasury and BOE may agree.
2. *Specifying the proportion of profit which may be credited to the reserves*: For instance, the Bank of Korea Act, 1997 has adopted an alternative approach by specifying the proportion of profits that Bank of Korea (BOK) may retain. It allows BOK to accumulate 30 per cent of the profits, after providing for depreciating assets, every year. It allows the balance

profits, remaining after such accumulation, to be credited to special purpose reserves, with the explicit approval of the Government. It mandates that the balance, if any, remaining after creation of such reserves must be paid out to the Government of Korea.

3. *Specifying the kinds of reserves that the central bank may accumulate*: The Bank of Thailand Act, 1942 specifically sets out the percentage of reserves that the Bank of Thailand (BOT) must accumulate. It requires the BOT to constitute the following reserves, namely, (a) ordinary reserves intended to cover possible loss; (b) reserves derived from the revaluation of assets and liabilities; and (c) other reserves for particular purposes as may be established by the BOT Board upon the approval of the Minister. The net annual profits of the BOT, after deduction of accumulated loss, if any, shall be provided in the following order for: (1) ordinary reserve amounting to 25 per cent; (2) other reserves for particular purposes, as specified by the BOT Board, upon the approval of the Minister. Any remaining net profits shall be paid in as state revenues.
4. *Capping the accumulation of reserves*: The United States follows a decentralised system of central banking where there is no single federal reserve bank, but 12 Federal reserve banks. The Federal Reserve Act, 1913, which governs the Federal Reserve System, mandates the Federal reserve banks to first pay out dividend to the stock holders (which are essentially member banks) in proportion to their holding in the Federal reserve bank. It then allows the surplus to be accumulated as a surplus fund of the Federal Bank, but specifically caps the surplus. It mandates that the surplus, if any, remaining with the Federal reserve bank, after providing for expenses, payment of dividend and allocation to surplus, shall be distributed to the Treasury.

The takeaway from the list of laws illustrated above is that there is a quantitative indicator that imparts clarity to the treatment of surplus assets by the central bank. The indicator may be indicative of what needs to be distributed, what needs to be credited to reserves or the cap on reserves. The RBI Act lacks this clarity, thereby leading to speculation.

Reserves Maintained by RBI

RBI maintains the following major funds: (a) Currency and Gold Revaluation Account (CGRA); (b) Investment Revaluation account (IRA); (c) Exchange Equalisation Account; (d) Asset Development Reserve (ADR); and (e) Contingency Reserve (CR). Out of these, the first three are funds to which unrealised gains and losses on existing assets of RBI, are credited and debited. The ADR was created out of profits to meet RBI's internal capital expenditure and invest in subsidiaries and associated institutions. The CR consists of the amounts added on a year-to-year basis for meeting all other unexpected and unforeseen contingencies (Malegam Committee Report (2013)). Therefore, technically, in the absence of any specific provision in the law, which restricts the internal capital expenditure that RBI may make or the contingencies that RBI can provide for, it is perfectly legitimate for RBI to credit the windfall to its CR or ADR.

In the absence of legal clarity, the Malegam Committee was set up by RBI to review the level and adequacy of internal reserves and surplus distribution policy of the RBI. It suggested that: (a) since the balances in the CR and ADR were in excess of the buffers needed, there was no need to make any more transfers to these funds; (b) the entire surplus should be transferred to the Central Government. Hence, for the three years immediately following the report of the Malegam Committee, i.e. 2013-14, 2014-15 and 2015-16, the entire surplus was transferred to the Government. This brought some consistency in the distribution of surplus. But, no steps have been taken to reform the law to ensure such consistency in future.

Conclusion

The present legal framework is unclear on the adequacy of reserves of RBI. While this has led to widespread speculation on what will happen to any windfall that may be realised from the demonetization event, the issue of distribution of surplus by RBI is not a one time problem. This problem will continue to crop up every time RBI has surplus profits. To ensure transparency in the distribution of surplus from the central bank to the CFI and to ensure the independence of the central bank in making such decisions, revisiting the legal framework governing reserves and the surplus distribution policy, is imperative. This legal framework should offer precise guidance on: i) the purpose for which the RBI can maintain reserves, ii) a cap on such reserves, and iii) the dividend distribution framework.

The last couple of years have witnessed some headway in reforming the decision making processes at RBI. In 2016, the RBI Act was amended to provide clarity on the manner in which it may exercise its monetary policy functions. The current government must focus its effort on such deep institutional reforms. It is a good time to resume this process by focusing on the decision making process for allocation of surplus assets by the central bank.

Source: *Legal Questions about Demonetisation* by Radhika Pandey and Bhargavi Zaveri, Ajay Shah's blog, 18 November 2016.

URL *https://ajayshahblog.blogspot.in/2016/11/legal-questions-about-demonetisation.html*